Dragons and Lions

My Life in Rugby

Dragons and Lions

My Life in Rugby

Steve Fenwick

with Craig Muncey

ST DAVID'S PRESS

Cardiff

Published in Wales by St. David's Press, an imprint of

Ashley Drake Publishing Ltd
PO Box 733
Cardiff
CF14 7ZY

www.st-davids-press.wales

First Impression – 2021

Paperback: 978-1-902719-85-6
eBook: 978-1-902719-91-7

British Library Cataloguing-in-Publication Data.
A CIP catalogue for this book is available from the British Library.

Typeset by Prepress Plus, India (www.prepressplus.in)
Cover designed by the Welsh Books Council, Aberystwyth

Contents

This book is dedicated to my family and friends who have helped me throughout my life.

Special thanks to Wendy, Kate and Siôn who have stood by me all the way.
I am very fortunate.
I love you loads.

Steve x

Preface

Steve Fenwick was one of the finest yet under-rated centres of his, or any, generation.

He showed very little emotion on the field, and this, I believe, helped him with his goal-kicking. A very laid-back person, Steve often pretended that he didn't train very much, although his teammates did not believe him! Remember, we all had jobs in the amateur era and we needed to motivate ourselves to train on our own as club training was often only a couple of hours on Tuesdays and Thursdays. For internationals, it was the Sunday before and a short run out on the Thursday! Steve most definitely had that motivation for training, but not so much for passing his driving test as for many years he relied on his friends and family for lifts to and from training!

At Bridgend, he was thoroughly trusted and always gave his all. His touch-kicking stretched the opposition and he often took over that kicking role, termed the second five-eighth in New Zealand, to enable the fly-half to focus on our running game. Steve was an extremely reliable goal-kicker and this helped Bridgend win the Welsh Cup in 1979 and 1980. The first cup win was, in particular, a fantastic achievement for us and very special for me, as it was our centenary year and I was captain. It was also special for us because, six months before, we had been kicked off the field by the All Blacks who'd visited the Brewery Field to mark our centenary. They certainly left their mark, but it wasn't for open flowing rugby – a huge scar across my face after an ugly stamping incident tore a hole in my cheek.

1979 was also an important time for Steve in the Welsh side, as Phil Bennett had retired the year before. As captain, I had no hesitation in giving the kicks to him, and he delivered time and time again. I don't think he had enough recognition for filling the kicking gap left by Benny, and playing his own game in the centre as well.

In 1981, I came out of retirement to play for Wales, and Steve and I were playing up in Scotland. The weather was awful, the pitch was muddy and, not many people know this, I was wearing experimental studs that were supposed to prevent skin lacerations. Whether it was the studs or the conditions, or both, but found it hard to keep my feet and slipped at a crucial moment when trying to gather the ball. I think Steve also struggled with his footing that day as well. Wales lost that day and both Steve and I were dropped, during Wales' much anticipated centenary year celebrations. It was hard to take so, to prove myself, I ran the first London Marathon and Steve switched to a successful new career in rugby league!

In 2020 the BBC ran a Greatest Five/Six Nations Try competition, and it was great that Benny's try from Scotland v Wales in 1977 had won, especially as lots of us had been involved in the move before Benny went over for the try. But who delivered the pass to Benny? The unsung hero, Steve Fenwick of course!

JPR Williams
Bridgend
July 2021

Acknowledgements

Looking back at my rugby career, I owe a lot of people an awful lot for the help and actions that got me to the pinnacle of my rugby prowess.

My auntie, Rose Childs, had the first television in Nantgarw, due to my uncle, George Childs, being the manager of Nantgarw Colliery, the biggest employer in the area. Rose was passionate about her rugby and she encouraged me, as a young boy, to watch international matches with her. She also played a role in my knowing how to sing *Hen Wlad fy Nhadau* as we all stood, side-by-side, in front of the television belting out the Welsh national anthem with immense pride. The first time I'd watched a Wales game with her she gave me a clip round the ear for not standing to attention for the anthem! I never made that mistake again. Rose and George were very kind to me and I appreciate the positive influence they had on my life. Their only son, also called George, was a good player in his own right and went on to play centre for Wasps RFC.

Gomer Richards was my PE teacher in Caerphilly Grammar School and developed my game as a schoolboy. He gave me the confidence to believe I could play for Wales one day, although neither of us were sure if I was going to win a cap playing centre or flanker. At the Welsh schools trial I played flanker and my first international game was at flanker for English Colleges against Welsh Colleges when I was a student at London's Borough Road College. It was only during the final year at college that I played centre. It worked and I remained there for the rest of my career.

Leighton Davies was the lecturer in Cardiff Teacher Training College who nurtured many future internationals from the college's conveyor belt. He was a huge influence at Bridgend RFC where he encouraged us to play open and expansive rugby. He also kept us in check if he felt we were getting too cocky and had several ways to bring us back down to earth.

John Dawes made a huge contribution to my career when he coached the Wales team from 1975 to 1980. As two uncapped centres coming into the world-class back line of Gareth Edwards, Phil Bennett, JPR Williams, Gerald Davies and JJ Williams, Ray Gravell and me were fortunate to play alongside such great players and to be coached by a master tactician. I was frightened stiff of trying to blend in with these incredible players, but 'Sid' Dawes instantly put us at ease by telling us to do, for Wales, exactly as we did for our clubs. Not only did we blend in so quickly and easily, I hit it off immediately with Ray and we became close friends, playing 20 games together for Wales.

Without the love and support of my parents, my sister and brothers, and my wife Wendy, I would never have been able to make the most of the opportunities that came my way. I also depended on Wendy's father, Bryn, my good friend Tom David and many others who patiently taxied me to and from training sessions for club and country. I owe them all a great deal.

Writing this book has brought back so many memories and it has been an absolute pleasure. I'd like to thank Craig Muncey, a good Nantgarw boy, for his assistance and to my former teammates and rugby friends: Derek Quinnell, Phil Bennett, Tom David, Phil Steele, Willie John McBride, Peter Squires, Gareth Jenkins, Gareth Davies, Lyndon Thomas, John Devereux and Gareth Rees for their generosity in contributing to my book and to Brynmor Williams for his Foreword, and JPR Williams for his Preface.

Steve Fenwick
Groeswen
July 2021

Foreword

It's not often you come across a character like Steve. He stands out in society because of his great success playing rugby, but he is also quite exceptional because of his warm personality and his ability to introduce humour into almost every aspect of life.

I had the pleasure of playing a lot with Steve and it was quite remarkable how he could puncture the tension in any situation. While it clearly helped his match-day preparation, it was also an advantage to his fellow players. I remember belly laughs in the Welsh dressing room ten minutes before kick-off because of something Steve had said or done.

Dressing rooms before international matches can be like funerals, such is the intensity of the occasion. One is almost desperate to lift the spirits and break the tension, with a laugh. Steve could be relied on to create normality with a down-to-earth and often funny comment to disperse the pressure-cooker atmosphere.

The stars who got the most attention in the 1970s were Gareth, Benny, Gerald and JPR. At the time they were the greats of the game on a worldwide basis. Each of them, though, will gladly confirm that they all depended on that powerful platform in midfield provided by SP Fenwick and the much missed RWR Gravell. Steve and Grav were key anchors in midfield as was David Burcher or David Richards, who both played several games when Steve or Grav were injured.

His contribution in the 1970s should not be underestimated. He seldom made a mistake in attack or defence, allowing the faster, perhaps more entertaining sidestepping players inside and outside, to shine. His unconventional goal-kicking was also instrumental in securing important results; and his "I'll have a go" approach was always refreshing in the cauldron of international rugby.

I still insist that the greatest conventional pass, under pressure, that I have ever seen was Steve's pass to Phil Bennett in a game against Scotland in 1977, when Benny scored one of the greatest, if not the greatest, Championship tries in history. It was poetry in motion and a technical example that should be used in every coaching film for youngsters or even current players in the modern game. It will sound to some people as if I am making a big thing about a simple pass, but it was a sign of a truly great player and I urge everyone who has not seen it to seek it out.

I travelled a lot with Steve, with Wales to Australia and Canada when Steve was captain, with the Barbarians to USA, and with the British and Irish Lions to New Zealand. He is a great friend, a companion and mentor. His warm personality and humour is always there, but never to the detriment of the team or the importance of the preparation. Yes, he could and would often be funny, but he knew when the focus had to be concentrated and complete.

It is a pleasure to support Steve's book. If ever there was a person who enjoyed his rugby, both the playing and the after-match festivities, it was most certainly Steve Fenwick. To his eternal credit he tried to make sure that everyone else did well.

Many players and coaches, both then and indeed today, take themselves too seriously, almost to the point that it inhibits their effectiveness. Steve never took himself seriously but he did take his rugby very seriously and this approach in conjunction with the warmth of his personality made him a player in-demand, and a person to be in and around high-level teams all over the world.

I am delighted to call Steve a friend. He is a very modest and an unassuming bloke, a respected and successful businessman, a seriously entertaining after-dinner speaker and more importantly, great company.

Brynmor Williams
Cardiff, Wales and British & Irish Lions
July 2021

Prologue

"JPR flattened by Carmichael. Fenwick. Gerald Davies - what was he doing there? And you can see, Davies, Phil Bennett, Bennett out to David Burcher. Burcher back inside to Fenwick, to Bennett. Oh, this is going to be the try of the Championship. That was absolute magic, and the whole crowd here knows it.

... Marvellous counter attack. Burcher did extremely well. The pass looked a little forward, but it was that marvellous quick pass from Fenwick that gave Phil Bennett that superb try."

Those were the wonderful words of the great Bill McLaren that so brilliantly described a memorable try from the Scotland v Wales international during the 1977 Five Nations Championship at a packed Murrayfield.

We had been under constant pressure from a good Scottish team for at least ten minutes when, defending another onslaught in our own half, JPR won the ball and popped it out to me. Our natural instinct was to attack whenever possible, without fear, and to use the skills and experience we had in our backline. We were confident without being cocky and we knew we were capable of anything, anywhere on the field.

Gerald called for the ball and I immediately sensed something was on. After taking the pass he majestically side-stepped two Scottish players and charged straight into midfield before planting a massive hand-off on their scrum half, Douglas Morgan. For a slight man, Gerald clouted poor Dougie and left him flailing, face down, on the pitch before passing the ball on to Phil Bennett who sprinted up the right-hand side of the field towards the halfway line. In support, as he always was, David Burcher had to check his stride in order that Phil could draw level with him and received the ball exactly on halfway. As David headed up-field, getting tighter with the touchline, I caught up with play and knew the next pass was coming to me.

Improvising a lovely, overhead, one-handed looping pass, I could see the Scottish defender about to pounce just as I caught the ball. It wasn't the dreaded 'hospital pass' but he was so close I could hear him as he rapidly closed in on me. I knew I had to move the ball on immediately, before getting clattered. Instinctively, in one movement, I caught then passed the ball back to Phil, who was close to my left. That night, at the official dinner, I was sat next to Bernard Wright, my former lecturer at Borough Road College who was by then working at Jordanhill College in Edinburgh. During the dinner he mentioned the try and, totally dead pan, said "You couldn't have possibly meant that Steve. It was obviously a fluke." I assured him, in no uncertain terms, that I most definitely meant it but I had realised that I only had a split second and couldn't afford any mistakes. It was arguably the quickest and shortest, yet most important, pass of my career.

Phil took the ball with just Sandy Carmichael, his good friend, left in defence. Fair play to Sandy, he had featured right at the start of the move, 'flattening' JPR as Bill McLaren had described, but he now faced Phil Bennett in full flight – an outside half against a prop – it wasn't a fair contest! As Benny side-stepped Sandy and the Scottish forward stumbled to the ground, grasping shadows, I can remember the prop forlornly muttering, "Ooh, you bastard Phil" as Benny headed for the posts to score that amazing try.

We won 18-9 and secured the Triple Crown for the second consecutive year, which was quite a feat, but it's the try that I am always asked about. In 2020 it was brought back into the public arena when it won a public vote, organised by BBC Wales, for the greatest Welsh try ever scored.

It was a great honour to play a part in the try and to still be remembered for it all these years later. We always endeavoured to play attacking rugby and that try encapsulated the very essence of what we set out to achieve. To play with such a talented team was a real privilege.

I've always been quite a laid-back person and writing my autobiography was never close to the top of my to-do list. I was far too busy playing rugby, running my own company and being the best husband and father I could. I hope you enjoy my journey through my career and my life. I have been very fortunate.

1

Wearing the Red Rose

'Steve was one of the outstanding centres of the 1970s. I have admiration for his rugby skills and physical strength, but also for his vision which aided him on the rugby field and ensured he played to the highest standards for so many years.'
Willie John McBride (Ireland, British & Irish Lions)

'I, Steven Paul Fenwick, have a revelation to make that may surprise many readers. My first international representative rugby union honours were playing for England, in 1972. There I was, in the line-up for the English national anthem with the red rose on my chest, representing English Colleges against Welsh Colleges. I know this may come as a shock and it still feels as odd now as it did all those years ago, but bear with me, don't judge me quite yet!'

As a teenager I played for Caerphilly Grammar School as a flanker, with the odd game at scrum-half, and I was also playing for Taff's Well RFC juniors, at outside-half and centre. I was playing to a decent standard – well, the standard must have been half decent as I was selected for a trial with Wales Schools held at Whitchurch Grammar School in Cardiff, in the 'probables' team, as an openside flanker.

Wearing the Welsh red shirt in a competitive game for the first time was a thrill and I saw this as my big opportunity to gain a Welsh cap and make my family very proud of me. This is what I'd dreamt of.

Alongside me in the back row on that memorable day in Whitchurch was a certain John Bevan, who was playing at eight. His powerful natural physique and deceptive speed gave him the ability to break tackles, which didn't go unnoticed. John would go on to be a massive success in both rugby union and league, and after one game at eight for Wales Schools, he was moved to the wing, where he never looked back. Also playing in that trial game was Jim Shanklin, on the wing, who would go onto win full international honours for Wales, and Bob Dyer, at scrum-half, who went onto play for Pontypridd for many seasons as well as for Swansea and Penarth.

The trial game went well for me, or so I thought. I scored three tries and was pleased with my performance. At the end of the game, one of the selectors came over to speak to me. I was fully expecting him to give me the good news about my selection for Wales Schools and to deliver some praise for my performance. However, that was not the case, and I will never forget the words he said to me: "I don't want you to be too disappointed, but you are not very big". Within seconds, as the shock and disbelief sank in, I replied the only way I knew and told him in no uncertain terms: "Well, I was big enough to score three tries"!

The reason for my non-selection soon became apparent. My main rival at openside for Wales Schools was Gareth Thomas, son of the acclaimed rugby journalist JBG Thomas, and it was he who got the nod to play at seven for the first international of the season. That game clearly didn't go well for him because, for the next international, he was moved to eight and then, for his third and his final Wales Schools appearance, Gareth was selected at prop. Three Wales Schools caps in three positions. If only my father had been a rugby writer or a selector: who knows, I might have got in! I believed I was a far better player than Gareth, no disrespect to him, but my Wales Schools knockback was certainly a big disappointment to me.

After my rugby disappointment I focussed my attention on my education and studied hard, passing 'A' levels in history, geography and economics. I'd already made my mind up that I wanted to get into teaching and to specialise in the teaching of physical education (PE). With with my exam results secured, I focussed on the five teacher training colleges with a good reputation for PE. In addition to Cardiff Training College in Cyncoed, Cardiff, I also liked the look of St. Luke's College (Exeter), Carnegie College (Leeds), Loughborough College

(Leicestershire) and Borough Road College (West London). Ultimately, I fancied a life change and living away from my familiar life in Wales was an opportunity that excited me, so I decided to go to Borough Road College and the bright lights of London.

Before being accepted onto the Borough Road College PE course, I had to undertake and pass a physical examination which consisted of tests in basketball, football, rugby union and gymnastics. I was very fortunate to have been spotted by Graham Rowlands, a fellow Welshman, who was captain of the college rugby union side and who also played flanker for Cross Keys at the weekend.

"What position do you play, Steve," Graham asked. "I've played flanker, centre, outside-half and can also play scrum-half", I replied. Suitably impressed, Graham then asked if I could "kick a drop goal", as one of the physical tests back then was to kick a drop goal. Because I had regularly practised kicking, not just with a rugby ball, but also with a football – for hours up against the wall from all types of different angles – I felt quite comfortable with my kicking ability. "Which foot?" I asked.

"You're fucking joking aren't you?" Graham shouted, before demanding a demonstration, so I proceeded to slot over two drop goals, one with the right foot and one with the left. Upon witnessing the two kicks, Graham immediately turned to the college's head of PE, a teacher called Bernard Wright, and said, "Get him in, we're having him!" I had an unconditional acceptance onto the course mainly due to my ability to kick a rugby ball!

It was quite an upheaval to move to the English capital, and being that distance from my family and also from my girlfriend at the time, and wife to be, Wendy, was tough at first. So was learning how to look after myself, from cooking to washing clothes, and it was, without any doubt, a steep and quick learning curve. I still kept in touch with friends and family and regularly travelled back and forth between my digs in Twickenham and my home in Nantgarw (between Cardiff and Pontypridd, near Taff's Well) by hitch-hiking, as I could not drive and the bus or train were out of the question for an impoverished student. Anyway, the exercise of running up and down roads trying to get lifts was a good exercise for my PE studies!

At the time, Borough Road College – which became West London Institute of Education between 1976 and 1995, before being subsumed into Brunel University in 1997 – was renowned more for producing top class athletes for track and field than as a conveyer belt for rugby players: St. Luke's and Loughborough, as well as Cardiff, were the rugby-playing colleges with the best reputations. Fortunately, for me, that would change over time, but the college introduced me to a wide array of sports including swimming, archery, judo, trampolining and gymnastics. I loved all sports and this suited me perfectly. I loved every moment learning many new sports and how to coach them correctly.

My newly-found access to so many new challenges brought me unexpected sporting success when I became the college's pole-vault champion! My fame was short-lived, however, when my personal best of 13 feet was beaten by a new student, Brian Hooper, who took the record to 17 feet 6 inches and went onto represent Great Britain in the Montreal (1976) and Moscow (1980) Olympics.

Brian wasn't the only star athlete to emerge from Borough Road during my time there. The college could also boast a number of talented athletes such as Alan Pascoe (400m), Alan Lerwill (triple-jump), Ian Green (100m) who, when at college, was the European champion, John Harrison (100m), Chris Monk (200m), and John Wilson (400m). A pretty impressive list, with some fantastic athletes. Brian would also go onto make a living in a very successful career in the TV show, *Superstars*, in which famous athletes from all over the world would compete against each other in several different sports.

I started playing rugby union for the college team in 1969 and the standard of rugby gradually improved thanks to the students being attracted to the three-year PE teaching training course. In addition, the team included some useful players who were studying to be teachers in other disciplines, from art to music and maths to science. We had enough players to field three teams and had many players to choose from.

Although we didn't play within the top echelon of English rugby, against teams such as London Welsh, Harlequins, London Irish or Rosslyn Park, our fixture list was of a good standard. Our opponents were teams such as Sidcup, Ealing, London Welsh 2nd XV, St. Luke's College, and Cardiff Training College: we had a decent side. The local derby was against St. Mary's College, which was also based in Twickenham. Another exciting fixture on the calendar was against the Metropolitan Police; students versus coppers – it was always a keenly contested match that one.

I was still trying to find my natural position and initially played at full-back, with several appearances in the centre alongside Nigel French, who would go onto represent England at a full international level, and with whom I would play alongside again in later life, in rugby league. I had made the switch from flanker because I was deemed to be too small to hold a place in the back row at the upper tiers of rugby union – size again had been my downfall! – but I did still get a few run-outs at six or seven. At the end of each season, we would go on a three-day tour to Cornwall and play Cambourne, Redruth and Penzance. It was a great tour and one we always enjoyed, with plenty of laughs and countless beers but we suffered it gladly and couldn't wait to go again.

We also were very good at sevens rugby. John Wilson, our 400m runner of some repute, was exceptional at several sports and with his extraordinary speed and endurance was tailor-made for rugby. At the Oxford Sevens competition in 1972, we played against Harlequins, and after John had run around his opposite number with ease and scored two quick tries, the somewhat exhausted foe asked me, "Who in hell is this guy?" I remarked that if he watched the Munich Olympics the following month, he would see John in the Great Britain 4x400m relay team!

During my final year, 1971-72, we also got to the final of the Middlesex Cup where we lost to Wasps 26-25. I scored all 25 points for the team, playing at, by now, my regular position, centre. At the end of that game, the Wasps coach approached me, asking what I was going to do at the end of my course. He thought I would be remaining in London as a PE teacher, and was trying to talk me out of joining London Welsh, assuming that was to be my likely choice of club.

London Welsh had several Welsh internationals on their books at the time, such as JPR Williams, Gerald Davies, John Dawes, John Taylor and Mervyn Davies; all great players. The Wasps coach pointed out to me that London Welsh had a centre called Gareth James in their ranks, who was highly regarded and he was not sure that, with Gareth there, whether I would get much game time. So, he pushed for me to come and play for Wasps. As it turned out, I had already applied for a teaching job in Bedlinog. At the time, I will be honest, I did not have a clue where it was, but the job application mentioned Glamorgan, so I

5

thought that would do! I got the job; otherwise, I could well have ended up playing for Wasps.

That Borough Road College team I played in was pretty decent. We had Ian Grocott at scrum-half, who did go on to play for Wasps; Gwyn Jones at outside-half who eventually played for Llanelli; Nigel French, who was capped at centre for England; Elgan Rees, a winger who went on to play for Wales and the British and Irish Lions; Rob Smith, a back-rower who played for England; and me. Also, in the back row, we had Bob Mordell, who before coming to the college had never played rugby union. Also a good goalkeeper, Bob would win his single England cap in 1978, against Wales at Twickenham, with me in the opposition ranks. John Harrison was the fastest sprinter in Europe in his age group, so it was no surprise that he was picked on the wing. To be honest, John was not that good a rugby player, just very fast! He ended up enjoying being captain for the 3rd XV and getting pissed pretty much every weekend after the match, some say during as well!

During my final year, when I was regularly switching between flanker or centre for Borough Road, English Colleges selected me to play for them against, wait for it, Welsh Colleges, at flanker! I was going to play against my own country and playing for, of all people, the English! Also selected that day to wear the red rose, was John Scott, who went on to play for Cardiff and England at lock, Peter Kingston, a scrum-half who played for England, and my back-row teammate at Borough Road, Bob Mordell. Welsh Colleges had some excellent players that day as well, including prop forward, Meredydd James and Tony Hodge, who had played for Wales – on the wing – as a schoolboy, but was now lining up at number eight for Welsh Colleges.

During the game, a lineout was called and as I was waiting for the ball to be thrown-in I heard the gruff voice from the Welsh player opposite me. It was Tony Hodge, who said, in a very matter of fact way, "You jump for this ball, and I will fill your face in." I did not fancy the sound of that, so I quickly turned and behind me at the back of the lineout was my old mate, Bob Mordell. Thinking fast, I said to Bob, "Can you switch places with me, Bob, as I can't see the ball coming in from here." Bob being Bob, such an amicable guy, did switch places with me with no hesitation, not knowing what may be incoming.

Anyway, the lineout happened without incident. Clearly Tony did not fancy his chances as much against Bob as he did against me!

Nonetheless, England went on to beat Wales, so I did not take too much stick from back home about who I was playing for seeing I was on the winning side. I did play a couple more times for English Colleges after that, in the centre of a very good team.

Many years later I discovered there was another person who had played for English Colleges against Welsh Colleges that day, who became famous in a very different walk of life. I was once at a rugby function, and my old friend and former Welsh international Ray 'Chico' Hopkins was there. Sitting next to Chico was Phil Serrell of BBC's *Antiques Roadshow* fame. Chico asked me if I knew the fellow sat next to him, and I replied, "Of course, I watch him quite regularly on television." They both started laughing; it turned out Phil played prop in that same England v Wales game, for the same team as me! Sorry Phil, but to this day I still have no recollection of you playing in that game, apologies! A former student at Loughborough College, Phil had got to know Chico through their shared interest in antiques. Chico is involved in buying and selling antiques as well as any other trades he can get involved into. One hell of a boy is Chico.

So, there you have it, my first representative honours were for England, but I would clean that stain of playing for the red rose quickly enough, and play for the country of my birth. I just hope you can all forgive me for that indiscretion at the start of my representative career!

2

Caerphilly Schoolboy

'Steve and I have been close friends since the mid-1970s. We were fierce rivals at club level but inseparable comrades in the red jersey of Wales. We both switched codes at the same time, and enjoyed playing rugby league for Cardiff and Wales. The two of us also also ran a successful business together after we retired from rugby. Steve was a talented centre and a tremendous goal-kicker for all the sides he played for. If I had to pick a team, Steve would be the automatic choice in my rugby union and rugby league teams. Our friendship goes on, both on the golf course, at functions, or in a local pub and long may it continue.'
Tom David (Wales, British & Irish Lions, Wales RL)

I was born in Caerphilly, in a house next door to the former girls' grammar school, on 23 July 1951, and was the third child born to my mum and dad, Margaret and John Fenwick. I have an older sister, Anne, who is the eldest, then there is Chris, my brother, then me and finally, born a few years later, was Mark, so my parents had four children in total. It was a lively and pretty chaotic household!

My first recollection of family life was when we moved to a brand-new Dyffryn Ffrwd housing estate in Nantgarw, which was a perfect area for parents with young families to bring up their children. Constructed on the the land that was originally part of the Dyffryn Ffrwd Manor, built by Sir James German in the 1920s, and now a nursing home, there were woodlands nearby, and the estate had an extensive area where children and families could play. There was also a huge orchard with many varieties of fruit trees, that was a magnet for the local children. The boys, in particular, enjoyed the old manor house's lake and streams which were full of trout and other fish.

We had such a wonderful time there as children and our family fell in love with Nantgarw, so much so, that my sister and brothers have remained in the area.

Anne spent much of her working life as a stewardess in the licensed trade at several well-known places such as The Lewis Arms in Tongwynlais, the Athletic Club in Rhydyfelin and The Halfway, on Cathedral Road in Cardiff. Anne was married to Ken Stephens, the brother of Ian Stephens, a prop for Bridgend, Wales and the British and Irish Lions. I have known Ian for many years, and you will hear a more about 'Ike', as he is known, later in this book.

Chris lives with his wife, Marsha and their children, a couple of miles away in Caerphilly. Chris and I share a love of rugby, and we both played with the same local rugby teams, Taff's Well and Beddau.

Mark still lives in Nantgarw with his wife, Caroline and their two sons. He was also a good sportsman and played rugby for Senghenhydd, Newport and captained Taff's Well. If I am honest, I always thought Mark was a better footballer, but the rugby route he decided to take was the one already well-trodden by the Fenwick boys.

Mark, Chris and I inherited our sporting genes from our parents, who were both passionate about sport and had considerable talent. My father, John, who was known as Jack to all his friends and family, came from Cadoxton, in Neath, and played rugby for Senghenydd. My mother, Margaret, hailed from Efail Isaf, a small village to the south of Pontypridd, and was a talented tennis player who was unbeaten for five years at her school, Pontypridd Girls Grammar. Both parents passed onto us the love and enjoyment of participating in sports, as well as their athleticism. We all have a lot to thank them both for.

Jack left school at 16, became a bricklayer and builder, and remained in the trade for the rest of his working life. He had a wicked sense of humour, another trait which all the Fenwick family inherited, and one particular incident – when Jack used me to get revenge on a pair of brothers – illustrates the point. The brothers used to play jokes on just about everybody who shared the same cabin for tea-breaks and lunchtimes, and Jack had decided to give them a taste of their own medicine by setting a trap for them.

Chris and I were regularly used as labourers to assist my father in his work but on this occasion it was just me working with my father, on a cottage by the canal in Nantgarw. We were removing an old lath and plaster ceiling during the renovation of the cottage when, to our amusement and surprise, a huge birthday cake covered in icing fell out of the ceiling. It was clear that the cake had been attacked by rats, mice and other creatures and was in quite a state, but Jack – you could almost see the cogs turning in his brain, a plan was very much afoot – decided to make it look presentable by cutting away the nibbled part .

The next day Jack let it be known that one of his sons was celebrating a birthday and he'd brought a large slice of it to work with him. He said it had been left in the cabin and, at lunchtime, if there was any left, he would share it with them. The trap had been set. Sure enough, almost immediately, as Jack and I were leaving the cabin to start work, you could hear voracious laughter from the brothers. They were gorging on the cake.

When lunchtime came, and we trooped back to the cabin, the brothers had huge satisfied grins on their faces. When Jack triumphantly produced the rotten half of the cake, infested with mice and rat bites and faeces all over it, the brothers barely made it outside the cabin to be violently sick. They never messed with Jack at work again. He was a hell of a character, my father.

My mother, Margaret, was fabulous. Nothing was too much trouble for her, even after having Jack and four children to feed and clean. The lasting memory I have of my mother was when she'd take me on our weekly pilgrimage, every Tuesday, to see my gran. My gran lived in a cottage opposite the Carpenters Arms in Efail Isaf. She always gave me tomato soup and, after that, I'd try and catch sticklebacks in the stream not far from the cottage with my fishing net. I have such happy memories of this. My mother, as well as looking after the family, had a job as a cleaner for Lloyds Bank on the nearby Trefforest Industrial Estate. Like everyone else, it's only when I look back do I fully appreciate all that was done for me in my early years by my mother.

My parents expected certain standards of behaviour from us, but were not strict disciplinarians. I can only recall one of them ever losing their temper with me. I was working alongside my father during the construction of the A470 in Rhydyfelin, when he was in charge of creating all the manholes. Two men had turned up for work the previous day and it had become evident to the site agent that, due to the poor standard of their work, that they were not *bona fide* builders. That morning, before we had even started our shift, Jack was dispatched to sort out the mess and, as he was leaving, Jack told me to go ahead and check-in our time cards at the machine. As requested, I went ahead and just after I'd checked us in, the timekeeper scrambled out of his cabin, shouting: "Instant dismissal!" The rules were that each worker could only check-in their own time card and no one was allowed to check others into or out of work.

I was pretty shocked, but I made my way back to Jack to tell him of his sacking! He was, unsurprisingly, furious. He had never been dismissed from any job in his life. Fortunately for me, on appeal, the site agent reversed the original decision and reinstated Jack. What a relief for him and, more to the point, me!

The Fenwick children were all pupils at Taff's Well Junior School, a small village school with a remarkable record of producing three British and Irish Lions: the great Bleddyn Williams, Ian Stephens and yours truly. My time at junior school sparked my love of sport, of all kinds, and gave me an excellent initial education. I have vivid memories of playing rugby at the school, in a lot of positions, initially at hooker. However, I was small in stature and it was a struggle in the forwards as I was way too small and light.

The boys were extremely competitive and we all wanted to play for the school rugby team, so I needed to find my best position. After experimenting at various positions I seemed to find my home at outside-half, mainly because I had started to develop a 'kicking game'. It was something I had established through many hours of practising with both a football and a rugby ball in the back garden and around the estate. I couldn't get enough of kicking a ball around and I'd only stop when my exasperated mother came out of our house and dragged me home.

The school field at Taff's Well was infamous for its 'dreaded slope', which started on the 25-yard line, furthest away from the school, continued over the half-way line and went all the way down to the try line. We had a secret weapon in our team, his name was Wayne Eldridge, and he came from Tŷ-Rhiw in Taff's Well. Wayne was nearly as big as our PE teacher, Mr Jones, and he was the only boy in our area who could kick the ball over the goalposts for conversions. The game plan was to kick the ball into touch on or close to the opposition's 25-yard line. Then, from the lineout which Wayne – due to his size – would usually win, we would all pile in on him and push him down the slope over the try line. It worked more times than not!

We must have had a decent side at school because we won the Cardiff Schools under-11s (with me as captain), the Cardiff Schools 7s tournament, and also played in the 15-a-side tournament on the old Cardiff Arms Park against St. Mary's School. The final ended in a thrilling 0-0 draw, which meant that the two schools shared the trophy, each having it for six months. The pitch for the final was far too big for boys of that age, so the whole game seemed to be between the two 25-yard areas, where two teams swarmed around the ball, like bees around a honey pot. However, the experience of playing at Cardiff Arms Park at such a young age was just fantastic.

There is one incident from my junior school rugby days that has stayed in my mind more than any other. Before kick-off in a match, we were called out of the changing rooms for a team photo. One of the lads, Gordon – who, like Wayne, also lived in Tŷ-Rhiw – made his way out of the changing room but his left leg went down a dirty drain which had no cover over it. As his leg splashed into the drain a jet of dirty water shot out all over his other leg and chest. The team photo clearly recorded for posterity, a sheepish Gordon with stinking muck all over his shirt and socks.

If I was not playing rugby, I was playing in and arranging football matches against local boys from Nantgarw, Taff's Well, Pontypridd, Pentyrch and anywhere else that would play against us. These matches were keenly contested, well organised, and were taken very seriously by those playing. I just loved kicking a ball around and no doubt playing all that football helped immensely with my development as a rugby player.

One of the biggest influences on me back then was my Aunty Rose. A huge rugby fan, she also lived on the Dyffryn Ffrwd estate in Nantgarw with my Uncle George and their Alsatian dog, Captain, who believed it was his duty to guard the estate. Captain terrified many a paper boy or a delivery man he didn't like the look of. I remember Aunty Rose inviting me to her house to watch a rugby match between Wales and England with her and my Uncle George, who was the manager of the Nantgarw Colliery. Compared to most people who lived in the area, they were wealthy people and were the first in Nantgarw to have a television.

So there I was, sat next to Aunty Rose, ready and excited to watch the match, when the Welsh national anthem started to be sung in the stadium. I was so enthralled to be seeing the spectacle on television I didn't see my Aunty Rose get to her feet to sing *Hen Wlad Fy Nhadau* so immediately incurred her wrath with a slap around the head. "Stand up for the anthem, Bach!" she bellowed at me. "How dare you sit down!" I learnt a lesson in manners that day that I'd never forget.

Aunty Rose was also the first person to take me to watch an international at Cardiff Arms Park. It was 1961 and Wales were playing England. I was nine years old and could not believe the atmosphere. It was fantastic. Little did I know then, that 14 years later I would be standing on the field playing for my country. Apart from the game, one thing that I distinctly remember from that day was the soaking we got from the shower which poured down on us from the North Stand as we stood the terrace. The odd thing was, it didn't actually rain that day, but the lack of toilets in the North Stand created a downpour I'd never forget! Even bearing all that in mind, it was still a fantastic experience and, thanks to Aunty Rose for taking me the Arms Park, it spurred me on to try and play for Wales one day.

As a schoolboy I used to deliver newspapers in the neighbourhood, which is how I first saw Wendy, my wife to be. Wendy used to go to Brownies in Nantgarw and I thought she looked very fetching in her outfit. I used to wave to her through the window of her house when I passed by on my paper round. One day I waved to Wendy as normal but after hearing screams from the house I discovered I'd actually waved at her sister! Clearly this case of mistaken identity did not turn Wendy against me and soon began to hang around with each other. Wendy's family lived in the first 'pre-fab' house, in Yr Hendre estate, by the pottery in Nantgarw. We have been in each other's lives ever since.

A big day for all junior school children in those days was the 11-plus exam, which dictated which secondary school you would go to. Living in Nantgarw, if I passed the 11-plus I could choose between Caerphilly or Pontypridd grammar schools, or, if I failed, it would have been a choice between the two secondary moderns in Trefforest or Trecenydd. Thankfully, I passed and opted to go to Caerphilly Grammar School, and it was a bit of an eye-opener for me. Everything was on a much bigger scale, and passing 'O' and 'A' levels was the priority. Alongside the emphasis on academic achievement, there was also room in the curriculum for a multitude of sports. The school had rugby pitches, and areas for athletics, both track and field, plus tennis courts and cricket pitches.

The school streamed the pupils into classes according to our level of academic ability, and I was placed into a class where the aim was to attain up to 11 'O' levels rather than the usual seven or eight at the time. Not for one moment did I think, before heading off the Caerphilly Grammar, that I would be studying Latin, Spanish and European History alongside Maths, English Language, English Literature, French, History, Geography, Economics, Chemistry and Physics! I cannot say that Latin or Spanish has been of any use to me whereas Woodwork and Metalwork certainly would have been. Wendy will undoubtedly agree with this as she is far more capable of fixing things around the house than me.

My initial fears of missing my school friends from junior school were not borne out as, along with making friends from around the Caerphilly area, I kept many of my existing friends such as Stephen Bowen and Brian Ware who had opted for Pontypridd Grammar School.

Caerphilly Grammar drew pupils from a wide area, and the social standing of the boys at the school was most obvious by our footwear. Those of us from Nantgarw, Abertridwr, Senghenydd and Llanbradach, the less-affluent villages, generally wore black footwear, known then as 'black daps', while those from Caerphilly itself, the more affluent part of the catchment area, who wore the more expensive 'white daps'. The difference was most noticeable after our respective daps had been cleaned and polished. Ours were pitch black while the 'posh boys' made the effort to whitened theirs.

My two best friends in grammar school were Michael Capelin and Geraint Watkins. We clicked straight away and have remained friends throughout our lives. Michael is from Caerphilly, and got up to all types of things, much of which he shouldn't have. Michael had a unique ability to be able to talk himself, or his friends, out of trouble. He has the priceless 'gift of the gab'. Being quite big in stature for his age, Michael made a good rugby player, usually played at number eight, and enjoyed a successful career in teaching, at secondary level, in Kent. Geraint is from Abertridwr and is the son of a former headmaster and Mayor of Caerphilly. He was also a decent rugby player. I count myself fortunate to have enjoyed Michael and Geraint's friendship.

Choosing a career was not the first thing on my mind, but as we approached the end of our school days, the discussions with teachers about our future plans started. On one occasion, Keith Davies, our History teacher who also took career lessons, quizzed me about my plans. I was doing well in his subject, and in most of my other subjects, and found it relatively easy to pass the exams. Based on my performance in class, however, he couldn't understand how I could be so successful. Fortunately for me, I had the ability to retain knowledge when revising just a short time before exams took place. He asked me my thoughts on a career, and I said I liked sport and teaching. The professional teacher paused and said, "I have got just the university for you when you leave, Fenwick." When I asked which university his immediate response was Karachi University, which puzzled me, so I asked him why that particular seat of learning? "Because that's as far enough away as I would like to send you!" came the reply. The discussion about careers ended on the spot with us all in uncontrollable laughter! As it happens, I did go into secondary level teaching and I taught, amongst other things, History, so my ability to retain knowledge must have continued!

My friend Geraint also had a similar experience with Mr Davies. When asked what career he wanted to get into, as quick as a flash Geraint, who was learning to play a variety of musical instruments such as harmonica, piano and guitar, replied: "I am going to be a rock star." Again, there was raucous laughter from the teacher. However, the last laugh was on him. Years later I was on holiday with Wendy in Turkey, and while we were in a bar I heard a familiar voice talking on the radio, it was Geraint. He had gone to America to perfect his art and had become one of world's premier exponents of the harmonica and an accomplished pianist and guitarist. In huge demand, Geraint played for, as a session musician or was invited on tour with, some of the biggest names in blues and rock 'n' roll such as the The Rolling Stones, Carl Perkins, Eric Clapton and Van Morrison. He's brilliant. If the name isn't familiar, look him up –

Geraint Meurig Vaughan Watkins from Abertridwr – you won't regret it. So, there you go, Keith Davies, don't say he didn't tell you he was going to be a rock star!

In his school days, Geraint had a bit of a temper and one lunchtime, when he had saved some money, a few of us went to Pino's Café at the top end of town, where Geraint bought a cream puff pastry he'd been looking forward to all morning. Outside the café we bumped into a small group of local lads, aged around 17-18, who were hanging around looking for trouble. They immediately noticed our grammar school blazers. It was like a red rag to a herd of overly aggressive bulls, and verbal jousting quickly turned into a bit of a scuffle. We may have been only 12 or 13 years of age but we stood our ground for a while before realising we stood no chance. Geraint was more concerned over the survival of his cream puff pastry and did his best to avoid getting involved – I think he would have preferred to have taken a few smacks to the face than lose his pastry – but his efforts were in vain as his pastry was soon splattered all over Pino's window and we decided the best course of action was to leg-it.

As already mentioned, Michael Capelin eventually moved Kent to become a Physical Education teacher, where he taught the England, and British and Irish Lions hooker Brian Moore. In his autobiography, Brian mentions that Michael had been his PE teacher, and had offered Brian some advice on his on-field temper and questionable behaviour. Michael had advised him to look to me as a role model as, my old school friend explained, I had been an uncontrollable, nasty idiot on the rugby field, and if I could curb my behaviour then surely, he could do it! That's a case of mistaken identity if ever there was one. If it were anyone else saying it I would have been upset but, fortunately, I know with Michael that you shouldn't take what he says too seriously. The principle of the story, although not the person, is spot on. He is a great lad and been a true friend for many a year.

It was with Michael's help that we managed to get a youth team off the ground in Taff's Well. At the time, the club was struggling to attract enough young players to field a team, so with the help of Stephen Bowen and Steve Parsons from Pontypridd Grammar School, and Nigel Poole, Michael and myself from Caerphilly Grammar School we agreed to play for our schools in the morning and Taff's

Well RFC Youth XV in the afternoon. The mix of players from the two schools created a formidable side. As schoolboys we couldn't get enough of playing rugby and loved doubling up for school and village.

My time at Caerphilly Grammar School was fabulous for academic study, but sports of all types were available to pupils who wanted to attain the very highest standards. The focal point was the PE teacher, Gomer Richards, who was excellent with the pupils. He treated them with respect, and we treated him the same. Another teacher who had a similar standing with pupils and the same ability to talk to them as an equal was our Maths teacher, Reuben Ballieux. He also was secretary of the Welsh Rugby Union's Welsh Schools set-up. The man loved rugby and could, at times, be quite overly serious and there were occasions when, if he saw us with a tennis ball or football, he would reprimand us for not playing with a rugby ball and then simply put a knife into the ball and confiscate it! The decrease in footballers coming out of Caerphilly over those years may have had a bit to do with Reuben Ballieux.

As I got older, my rugby abilities developed and when I was around 14 or 15 my physical stature changed and I became taller, more muscular and heavier. I think this was due to the work I was doing as a labourer with my father, and also taking part in athletics and other sports in school. I also started going to a gym where I became aware of the importance of having a healthy physique, which played a massive part in my career. However, it was not until I was 16 or 17 years of age that I developed the physique and levels of fitness that I wanted. The academic side of my education was going well so I was quite a happy schoolboy.

There was, though, one incident in school that really did have an impact on me. It was all over a silly prank that went wrong, involving myself and a lad called Gareth Thomas. It started when at a break time when we were amusing ourselves, as teenagers do, playing the age-old game of running the concrete cricket roller across the tennis court and flattening some poor pupil's shoes into the ground (surely everyone did this?). However this time it turned sour. We lost control of the roller, and it headed towards the tennis court fence with only myself and Gareth trying to bring it to a halt. We failed, and it smashed through the fence before careering down a large embankment onto the athletics track, which was approximately 100 feet below. To our horror, the French teacher, Neil Harris, and his assistant were on the track, marking out the lanes. The roller hurtled across the track and, luckily, didn't hurt anybody as it could have been far worse with serious injuries. The school prank that certainly backfired on myself and Gareth.

Once he'd composed himself from the shock, Mr Harris marched us both off to the headmaster's office. At the time I was sure he wanted our expulsion from school, at the very least, but what we got was a severe lecture on our conduct that day and our future behaviour. I also ended up as the only player from the 1st XV not to be made a school prefect, but that was still not enough punishment and I had to suffer another penalty which really hurt me. Our school had an annual rugby fixture with Lycée Lacanche, a school in Paris, which we all looked forward to immensely. This is where Mr Harris came into his own. As a French teacher, and being in charge of the school rugby team that year, he took charge of the trip to Paris so had *carte blanche* to do what he liked. He announced that I was dropped from the team. It was the first and only time I had been dropped from the school team, and I could only think that the cause was down to the roller incident. My place in the team was taken by a boy called Martin Harris (no relation to Neil), who was now on his way to Paris as a last-minute call-up and could not believe his luck. I was still allowed to travel to France, but it was made crystal clear that I wouldn't be playing.

Or that was the plan. Somehow, on the day of the match, a twist of fate gave me a helping hand as Martin Harris had unfortunately been stuck in the Parisian traffic on his way to the ground, and missed the kick-off. As a result, and to his great annoyance, Mr Harris had to put me in the side as a replacement. The, as luck would have it, I came on and scored two tries that helped us win the game by six points to three. Mr Harris, for the remainder of the trip, refused to acknowledge or mention my contribution to the win but, in my view, justice had prevailed!

The group of players in my year at Caerphilly Grammar School stayed together as a team from under-13 to under-18 levels and during that time we were quite successful as a side. We lost very few games, and we were playing the best teams in Welsh schoolboy rugby including Pengam, Neath, Haverfordwest and Whitchurch. Playing in these games, and doing well, no doubt helped in my progression to being selected for trials at a national level even if the outcome was not as I'd hoped.

I had a great childhood and enjoyed my school days, and I count myself to be very blessed to be able to say that.

3

Taff's Well RFC
1970-72

'A legendary figure to all of us at Taff's Well RFC, Steve Fenwick has always been a good friend to the club where he started his career. From the boys and girls playing mini-rugby through to the youth and senior teams, every generation of rugby player has been inspired by what Steve achieved for Wales and the Lions, knowing that it all began at Taff's Well.'
Gareth Rees (Chair, Taff's Well RFC)

I've enjoyed a long and happy relationship with Taff's Well RFC, from playing junior rugby through to senior level with the 1st XV. Initially, I watched my brother, Chris, playing flanker for the youth team, and loved it so much I started to follow the team – home and away – on a Saturday afternoon. It wasn't long before I stopped watching and started playing.

Our youth team was pretty good and we had quite a successful period, winning most of our games in some style by playing open, attacking 15-man rugby. We also won the Pontyclun 7s tournament, outperforming the tournament favourites Llanharan RFC, which surprised many of the local rugby establishment including the Chairman of Pontyclun RFC who was the Master of Ceremonies for the trophy presentation. We all fell about laughing when he announced that Llanharan RFC were the tournament winners. He quickly corrected himself, called us up and awarded the trophy to Taff's Well Youth team.

I also played for Taff's Well when I came home from college at the weekend, and outside of the academic year, but only for the 2nd XV as the club had a ruling that students who lived away could not play for the 1st XV, in order to maintain a regular, consistent side. I guested for the 2nd XV on numerous occasions and enjoyed the involvement with some of the senior members of the club, and it was character building, to say the least.

I was only around 16 years old when I started playing for the 2nd XV and, being so young, I was soon targeted by opposition players. The team countered this by making my teammate, Keith Mapstone, or 'Twitto', my minder. He was a hardened rugby man who had played for Pontypridd earlier in his career, before playing for Taff's Well with great distinction for many years. He was a man of few words, but he was lethal as my minder and if anyone was considered to be taking advantage of my inexperience they had Keith to deal with! If I was being harassed or fouled during the game, all I had to do was give Keith the shirt number of the player who was bothering me, and as if by magic, that player would be neutralised by Keith, our 'silent assassin'. He certainly lived by the maxim that actions speaks louder than words.

In those days the 1st XV and the committee men travelled to away games by a luxurious (by 1960s standards) coach, leaving us lot in the 2nd XV to make do with other, less impressive, modes of transport! I recall one game against Nantyffyllon RFC when we organised the whole team – 15 players as there were no replacements in those days – to travel in a convoy of four cars. We set off together from Taff's Well but when we arrived in Nantyffyllon, near Maesteg, we discovered that one car was missing. Unconcerned, we trooped into the clubhouse to get changed, assuming the final three players would be arriving shortly.

By the time the game was due to start our teammates were nowhere to be seen, and when the referee knocked on the changing room door and told us to come out for kick-off we knew we were in for a challenging afternoon. We delayed a bit further but the 'Taff's Well 12' eventually emerged and set up with six backs and six forwards. Unsurprisingly, we were under severe pressure from the kick-off with Nantyfyllon showing no mercy whatsoever for our under-strength team. Taking no prisoners they came straight for us and we were soon six points down.

After about 15 minutes, and under continuous pressure, we suddenly noticed the missing car with the AWOL players pulling up by the side of the pitch. The 'Taff's Well 3' jumped out of the car, undressed and kitted up right there before sprinting straight onto the pitch. This gave us such a boost that we were able to push on and gain an unlikely victory. Michael Green famously wrote about the *Art of Coarse Rugby*, and that was how it felt playing for Taff's Well!

On the few occasions I did play for the first team, you could sense it was a step up from the the seconds. It was harder – physically and mentally – with a more structured game plan, but still great fun. The highlight of the season was always the local derby match with our near neighbours up the hill, Pentyrch RFC. Winning that game and holding the local bragging rights until the next encounter was essential, and everyone looked forward to it. On one occasion, after several late tackles – only to be expected in a local derby – an incident of mistaken identity occurred.

Chris, my older brother, and me were both playing for Taff's Well that day. I was playing outside-half, and he was at flanker. Both teams flew into each from the start and a few naughty tackles were going in. As tempers flared, the referee stopped the game and gave a general warning to both sides that a sending off was likely if those types of challenges did not stop. The Pentyrch outside-half, a lad called Fred, had been in the thick of the action and had been responsible for a few late tackles. By now, I was absolutely seething.

Five minutes later, and despite the referee's warning, I saw my opportunity to give Fred a taste of his own medicine: a late tackle, which the referee luckily only caught a brief glimpse of. Well it was lucky for me, but not for my brother. The referee immediately stopped the game, ordered Chris over to speak to him, and promptly sent him off! Chris and I do look very much alike and everyone apart from the referee realised what had happened. Chris was livid, I kept quiet and the Pentyrch players found the whole thing highly amusing.

After much pleading with the referee Chris left the field but then threatened to kill me if I did not tell the referee that it was me not him who was responsible for the foul play. Every now and then during the game I could hear him remonstrating on the touch line that I was going to be killed by him at the end of the game. Eventually, after much discussion between several of the players and the referee – with Chris loudly making his feeling know from the side lines – the referee finally allowed him back onto the field, which no doubt saved me a hiding afterwards!

The 2nd XV had a real mix of players, from non-achievers dropped from the first team and players who were approaching the twilight of their careers but still had a lot of experience, to the ambitious younger boys who were eager to learn and had their eye on the 1st XV. As one of the younger contingent, it was great to be around these older players and it proved to be exhilarating on and off the field. It was pure enjoyment to be pitting your wits with your colleagues on the rugby field, and some of those characters I will never forget.

One such character was Clive Day, a Taff's Well man through and through, who I remembered playing in his heyday on the old pitch, where the village's soccer team now play. The 1st XV had a good side and was unbeaten at home for several seasons. A lot of their success was due to Clive's game management from outside-half. He was very skilful and fully committed to the cause, and although his approach differed a little in the 2nd XV, his sense of humour kept his teammates in stitches on and off the field.

I first got to know Clive and the rest of the players through playing games and training at the club. Clive was also instrumental in getting me the best job I ever had, while I was still in college, when he secured a 'job' for me one summer holiday at Port Talbot steelworks with his work gang. I say 'job' because I never did a stroke of work for six weeks, and on a Sunday, it was double pay! What a great summer that was! All I had to do was put a spanner in my back pocket, wear a helmet and, as Clive instructed, just walk around the vast site. If anybody stopped me or asked me who I was, I was told to reply, "Temporary AEU" (AEU was the Amalgamated Engineering Union). I was a 'temporary' union official, and that was my passport to freedom.

I was told by Clive to report to the canteen at break and lunchtimes and to be ready to leave the site promptly in the Taff's Well contingent's van to get home early, just to rub it into the other workers. 'Working' on a Sunday earned us double pay, but all we did was clock-in, then go through the hole in the fence and head straight to the nearby Naval Club where we stayed all day watching the strippers perform on stage and get pleasantly sozzled. When I eventually got home to my parents, I'd be very much the worse for wear and I would be in bed by 6pm. My poor mother expressed her concern to my father that I was working way too hard, was worn out and that I should take it easy! Little did she know, and she would have been extremely embarrassed with the truth of the matter, although I don't think my father thought I was working too hard, especially on a Sunday. I think he had more than an inkling of what was going on!

While playing for the 2nd XV I was usually selected at outside-half especially after Clive had moved to full-back for a quieter time. A certain John Peter Rhys (JPR) Williams was, however, changing the role of full-back play to more of an attacking role, rather than a defensive position deep inside your half, and Clive's wish was soon to be shattered. JPR had a lot to answer for from many a defensive full-back at all levels, including Clive.

As I eased into the role of the team's regular outside-half I increasingly set the ethos by which I wanted us to play. Before one game I told the backs – with Clive clearly audible muttering obscenities from the full-back position – that if we got possession from a scrum or lineout, I would be looking to run the ball at almost every opportunity. For the next phase of possession I called a move in which we would miss out one of the centres and feed Clive the ball in midfield, and we would support his burst up field. When we quickly checked with Clive what was he going to do when he got the ball, his reply was a classic: "Give me the ball, I'll put my head down and my arse up and see how far I can go", which brought guffaws of laughter from the players on the field!

Clive also had a thing about disappearing from the pitch during play. During the second half of a game against Llandaff North 2nd XV on our pitch at Ynys, the opposition outside-half decided to kick over the top of our three-quarter line, and we turned to see how Clive – as our last line of defence – would deal with the situation. However, to our horror, there was no Clive! We quickly scuttled back and managed to get the ball into touch, out of danger.

All of a sudden the players burst into laughter when they noticed Clive – through the clubhouse window, around 20 yards from the side of the pitch – enjoying a pint of bitter! Having incurred the wrath of the referee, Clive was ordered to return to the field, and as he ran back onto the pitch, the referee called him over and told him it was sending off offence to leave the pitch without permission during play. "Now wait a minute," said Clive. "If I don't turn the spuds down in the oven, there will be no food for the players after!" The referee could not help breaking out in giggles with the rest of the players, and we just got on with the game.

He repeated his dash to freedom at the end of the same season, away to Llantwit Fardre 2nd XV. It was a warm evening, and the match was in a bit of a lull when they broke through our first line of defence, the full-back was nowhere to be seen, and so they cantered over for an easy try. We were under the posts waiting for the conversion when we noticed our full-back leaning on an ice-cream van near the touch line! Clive was thoroughly enjoying his ice-cream in the warm weather as he raised his hand and gave us the thumbs-up. What a fantastic character he was. Sadly Clive is no longer with us, and he is sorely missed.

David Owens, who played on the wing, was another character at the club, who would keep you thoroughly entertained on and off the field. Once, while playing for the 1st XV, I was a touchline spectator when Dai and his opposite number had a bit of 'handbags at dawn' when, as they chased the ball into touch the shoving quickly escalated. The opposition winger told Dai, in no uncertain terms, that if he did that again punches would fly. Dai responded by saying he would keep the lad up in the air with repeated uppercuts, at which the referee nearly fell over laughing as did the rest of the players, including Dai's opposite number.

Billy Symonds was another winger of note and a great servant to the club, he was never short of a word or two. He was also a deep thinker of the game. I watched a game at Ynys where Billy got embarrassed by the opposition winger zooming around him on the halfway line and scoring under the posts. The Taff's Well captain, surprised by the lack of an effective defence, challenged Billy as to why he had not chased the winger from the halfway line and tried to prevent the try? Quick as a flash, Billy replied that he had been stung by a bee! "What, in January?" The captain said to Billy, "I don't fucking think so Bill!"

Almost all of the youth team players I grew up with retained their links with Taff's Well RFC in one way or another, either as a player or in a social role with the club. It is a great club with great tradition, and a period I look back on with great fondness. The Taff's Well RFC team of the mid-1970s certainly put the village on the map, with their expansive rugby led by Elwyn Williams, one of the brothers of the great Bleddyn Williams. The Williams boys; Bleddyn, Elwyn, Bryn, Lloyd, Tony and Vaughan, were all superb rugby players and all born in Taff's Well itself. Has there ever been so much rugby talent in one family? I don't think so.

In 1973, Taff's Well drew Swansea RFC in the WRU Cup to set up a mouth-watering home tie. Swansea had plenty of internationals playing such as Mervyn Davies, Trefor Evans, Geoff Wheel, Barry Clegg and Roger Blyth to name but a few. It was an epic contest with Swansea edging home by 13-6.

The following season Taff's Well RFC once again grabbed the media headlines, when the team was drawn at home against Llanelli in the WRU Cup. Llanelli was blessed with an abundance of playing, stars such as Ray Gravell, Roy Bergiers, JJ Williams, Derek Quinnell and Gareth Jenkins so we knew we were in for a huge afternoon. It is to the great credit of Taff's Well that they gave Llanelli a real fright, eventually losing 10-6. Llanelli went on to win the cup that season, which illustrates what a good performance it was by Taff's Well to push them that close. It was an exceptional effort by a proud and resilient Taff's Well team.

I will be forever grateful that Taff's Well RFC gave me an opportunity, from youth level up to a senior level, to play and enjoy rugby. There is a real rugby tradition at this proud village club, which has produced six Welsh internationals, three Welsh captains and three British and Irish Lions to date, a pretty impressive record. Being part of that rugby heritage fills me with great pride. Up the Well!

4

Caerphilly Schoolteacher

'Little man, big heart'
Terry Cobner (Wales, British & Irish Lions)

After graduating with a degree in physical education, my career as a teacher started in Bedlinog, a mining village between Pontypridd and Caerphilly. I must admit, though, that before applying for the position I had no idea where Bedlinog was!

My application to the junior school must have interested them as I was invited for an interview. After discovering where Bedlinog was and making my way there, I was greeted by an interview panel of eight people, including Dilwyn Maddocks, the headmaster, some school governors and a few others. I was very nervous and fixed my eyes on the headmaster, but as we got going and I began giving my responses to their questions – my confidence growing by the second – I started looking around the panel and noticed that four of the eight were knitting, paying no attention at all to the proceedings!

That lack of interest dented my confidence somewhat, so when I was offered the job, I was very surprised. I did find out afterwards that there had been nine applicants for the position: eight graduates from the Cardiff College of Education, in Cyncoed, and me from Borough Road, London, so maybe they just wanted someone with a different view of the world.

It was a typical village school, and I had around 20 boys in my year to teach. I hadn't learnt to drive at that time so getting into work each day was a bit of a journey. I had to catch the bus from Tongwynlais, where I was then living, to Ystrad Mynach, followed by a lift to Bedlinog, and the same journey home after work. By then I had moved from Taff's Well RFC to play for Beddau RFC, a few miles in the opposite direction towards Llantrisant, and needed to get to training after school, either at the club or by going for a jog on my own. It was a busy time, but I enjoyed being a teacher and my my rugby was improving.

In the years before I joined the staff, Bedlinog School had downgraded rugby union as the main sport and it wasn't played that often. I immediately changed that and reintroduced rugby back into the school, and we built up quite a good side, beating Pengam and other local schools, known for being rugby specialists. The children enjoyed their success and I gained a lot of satisfaction from seeing my efforts being rewarded.

I regularly took the boys down to the playing field in the village for a training session and, on the way back, while they went on ahead on their short walk back to the school, I had a pint of shandy at The Railway Inn. Handily located on the square in the centre of the village square, the landlord and I had an understanding, and he would leave a pint out for the thirsty teacher. I loved my time there. They were great days!

I have been back to Bedlinog several times over the years for different functions, and it is great to see that many of those boys I trained went onto play rugby for the local village side or nearby villages such as Nelson RFC. It is a good feeling to know that they enjoyed their rugby and continued to play after leaving school.

Unfortunately, after just one year at Bedlinog Junior School, local government restructures due to the introduction of comprehensive education meant that several schools were amalgamated and I was faced with moving to a new school. Luckily I had three options: Pengam in the Rhymney Valley, Afon Taf, in Troed-Y-Rhiw near Merthyr, or St. Cenydd in Caerphilly. Purely based on location, and the fact I couldn't drive, I chose St. Cenydd. I could now catch a bus from Tongwynlais to Caerphilly and it was then a short walk (or run, as I did for a bit of morning training), to the school.

Caerphilly's St. Cenydd Comprehensive School's catchment included children from Senghenydd, Abertridwr and Nantgarw, so the indicator of social class I'd noticed as a school boy, the black daps v white daps divide, was obvious. Discipline was a big issue in the school, and I certainly would have my hands full, particularly as a new teacher in a type of school where children would definitely test boundaries. The headmaster, a gentleman called Basil Phillips, welcomed me in as their new PE teacher, and I appointed as assistant to the head of the PE Department, Islwyn Gray.

I was still at the bottom of the teachers' pay scale, money was limited and it was quite challenging, financially. Wendy and I had got married in 1972, in Nantgarw and, with Wendy training to be a nurse and me as a recently qualified teacher, times were tough but we consoled ourselves with the knowledge that there were plenty worse off than us. I was certainly kept busy during those days, taking the boys for rugby training at lunchtime, after school, and Saturday mornings.

I'd like to think that I was hard-but-fair as a teacher, and I knew I was making progress when, one day, I saw 'Fenwick is a Bastard' daubed on a school wall. 'You are earning their respect now, boy', I thought to myself! I recall one time when one of the boys who got himself into trouble quite frequently came to one my PE classes with no kit. I wasn't happy and told him in no uncertain terms to make sure he had his kit for the next PE class. Sure enough, the next time, he turned up again with no PE kit. I asked him why but the boy offered no excuse, so I told him he was going to do PE in just his trousers and braces. You should have seen the state of him!

The following day during one of my lessons I was summoned to the headmaster's office, and sitting there was the father of the boy who had turned up without any kit. The father was the owner of a local business, and he was seething. In his view I had embarrassed and humiliated his child. I told him exactly what had happened, and he still was not happy, making all kinds of threats including getting me dismissed. Eventually, I told him that if was still unhappy, he could come and meet me any day at 3.45pm when I'd be more than happy to 'discuss the matter with him'. He never did come to see me, and threats of the sack never materialised. He clearly thought he could, as a local businessman, throw his weight around but I felt I was in the right and defended myself, which sometimes you have to do.

At St. Cenydd's we built a good rugby team which became quite successful against local schools. Seeing the boys playing well and winning often was very satisfying, but the abuse I used to take from parents and teachers from opposing schools when standing on the sidelines made me ask myself if it was all worth it. It got so bad that Wendy asked me why was I suffering all this grief while still at the bottom level of the pay scale. I concluded that, from a rugby perspective, it was still rewarding as a number of the pupils went onto play first-class rugby in Wales, but I did understand where Wendy was coming from.

As the years went by I started teaching History and Geography, as well as PE, which suited me as I really enjoyed history, and still do. I will never forget one answer to a test I set around the topic of Stonehenge, which the class had been studying. One of the questions asked, 'What was the purpose of Stonehenge?' I was looking for the pupils to provide the answer that it was a burial site, or used for rituals and ceremonies. "To keep the sheep in", came a response. How big did this boy think these sheep were?, I thought.

Before long, Liberal Studies was added to my teaching portfolio. Initially, I had no idea what it was but, after a few lessons I realised it was a subject where all the trouble makers that other teachers couldn't handle, were grouped together, for me! I used to tell them to open their books and get on with any work they wanted, but to keep quiet. It seemed to work! I'd now been teaching for a few years but was still on stage one of the pay scale. My frustration was starting to build, and it was all to come to head pretty soon.

By now I'd moved from Beddau RFC and was playing first class rugby for Bridgend, and had been capped for Wales, so I was travelling extensively. I still hadn't learnt to drive so I came to rely, more and more, on poor Wendy for lifts, which was putting pressure on us with our working schedules. For Welsh training sessions in Aberavon, I used to travel with Tom David, and he had mentioned to me a few times about leaving teaching and going to work with him and Derek Quinnell at Gremer Chemicals, where they both were sales representatives. Jimmy Scoular, the ex-Cardiff City manager, was also working there, and the owner of the company was eager to get me onboard. It was very tempting: better money, more flexibility with the working hours and Wendy and I were keen to start a family. With these thoughts in mind, I decided I had enough, I was going to approach the headmaster, Basil Phillips and ask for a pay-rise, after seven years of teaching: I justified it. I rehearsed my speech that I was going to deliver, I was ready.

CAERPHILLY SCHOOLTEACHER

The day of my meeting with the head dawned and I walked into his office, which had the blinds down even though it was bright and sunny outside. Basil Phillips was smoking a pipe, working on his typewriter. Thick tobacco smoke filled the room, which added to the sinister atmosphere for what I was about to do. I delivered my speech and thought it had all gone very well, so I awaited the, hopefully, positive response. After a long few minutes of silence, Basil looked up and delivered a short statement, "Well, Mr Fenwick. You've got to move on to get on. Please shut the door on the way out!"

With his verdict delivered, it was clear my teaching career of seven years was at an end. I had really enjoyed teaching, but I felt massively undervalued, and with my family plans, I had to make a change. I needed a change of career.

After three years in teacher training college, and seven years as an educator, it was a big upheaval for me and a bit of a gamble for the people who took me on in a role with no experience: an industrial sales role, which meant a lot of travelling, and meeting different people to establish new contacts and hopefully, new business. I was still a non-driver but, thankfully, for me and for Wendy, her father, Bryn, was my saving grace. He sacrificed his own time to join me in the car, displaying my L plates, while I drove to appointments. Bryn and I were a great team and I was so thankful to him for his patience and support at that time. Luckily for Bryn, I quickly passed my test which meant I no longer required his presence in the car and he could go back to enjoying his retirement. Wendy and Bryn sacrificed a lot for many years to ensure I was where I needed to be, and they weren't the only ones. Many poor souls provided me with lifts and I'll be eternally grateful to them all, including Lyndon Thomas and Tom David.

It was great fun working alongside Jimmy, Derek and Tom at Gremer Chemicals. There was plenty of banter, especially considering that Tom was playing for Pontypridd, Derek for Llanelli and me for Bridgend so, dependent on results from the weekend, you could be the butt of the jokes or dishing it out to the others. After around a year with the company, Derek raised the idea of him, Tommy and me going into partnership on our own. The idea quickly grew and gained momentum, and, in 1979, we finally decided to leave Gremer Chemicals, and go into business together.

Naming our new company wasn't a difficult task. Wales were enjoying a golden era of success, so with three fellow rugby internationals now becoming business partners, Triple Crown Chemicals, an industrial supply company, was born. We registered the business name, set up a bank account and sorted out premises, in Brackla, near Bridgend. We were all set.

However, there was to be a late change to the plan. At the last minute, Derek pulled out of the partnership, which left just Tom and me. We could not change the name, as it had been registered, so we continued with Triple Crown Chemicals. Our understanding of running a business was negligible, but sales slowly started to grow, with our rugby contacts playing an essential role.

One of our first contracts was with Jim Powell who worked for Beddau Coke Works. When Tom and I went to meet him, Jim asked all the pertinent questions such as which chemicals we used, what was their flashpoint, and what kind of temperature would it generate underground etc. All great questions, but this was certainly not our speciality. I looked puzzled, and Tom just looked at the ground. I finally admitted to Jim, that we were struggling to answer his questions. He just looked at us and said: "Don't worry boys, no Welsh international has ever walked out of this office without an order," which was a relief to say the least!

It was around this time that Tom and I started playing golf regularly, usually with a great friend of ours, Chris Beacher. We enjoyed each other's company and had a great time on and off the course at Pontypridd Golf Club, and any other course that was willing to have us. Quite a few of the rugby fraternity also enjoyed their golf, such as Gareth Edwards, Gareth Davies, Brynmor Williams, David Richards, Malcolm Dacey and Derek Quinnell to mention just a few. Some of the Scottish rugby boys were also excellent golfers. Dougie Morgan was a 'scratch', no handicap, professional-level golfer, and Gordon Brown was about a five handicap. So whenever we were together, and rugby allowing, we would seek out a golf course.

If you played with Dougie Morgan, his handicap was a can of beer he had to drink for every hole we played. So after about nine holes, Dougie, ability-wise, was on about a par with the rest of us. I remember Charlie Faulkner and Bobby Windsor joined us for a game of golf in Australia when on tour there in 1978. Charlie took three attempts at hitting the ball off the tee on the first hole. He then stated that golf was not as easy as it looked, whereas Bobby, also on the first tee, asked the amused spectators, "Which one of these sticks do I use on the first hole?" Bobby then proceeded to hack his way around the golf course and, if in a spot of bother, he would often use the 'leather wedge', in other words, his shoes, to gain a good position for his next shot. Well played Bobby!

With the business growing, and with sales going strong we took on more staff to help with the orders. One of those new recruits was my brother, Chris who joined us as sales and factory manager. We then moved premises from Brackla to Ystrad Mynach, which made the travelling easier for Tom and me. We took on customers in not just southern Wales as we'd hoped, but across to west, mid and north Wales, as well as the Bristol area. We also expanded into the painting of factory floors as well as selling the painting products to other companies. We all got stuck in to finish the projects as soon as we could, especially with me, Tom and Chris needing to complete the contracts so we could concentrate on playing rugby on the weekends. It was hard work, but great fun.

We eventually sold the company at the end of the 1980s. Chris went into business in the same industry, and Tom and I both went into industrial recruitment, which I am still involved in to this day. Tom has been a great friend for many years and I couldn't have wanted a better or more loyal business partner.

5

Beddau RFC 1972-73

'On and off the field there was no fiercer or more determined competitor.'
Brynmor Williams (Wales, British & Irish Lions, Wales RL)

The switch to Beddau RFC came about after a match I'd played against them for Taff's Well 2ⁿᵈ XV. The game, in Beddau, came at a time when they had not lost at home for some time. On that day, however, they lost, and I had played well. After the game, a member of the Beddau club was chatting to me and asked asked why I was playing for the seconds when I was so much better than that. He then invited me to join the club, where I'd go straight into their 1ˢᵗ XV. I'd felt for a while that I needed a new rugby challenge, and to play at a higher level would aid my progression so the move made total sense. My brother, Chris, also made the move to Beddau RFC and we had great times both on and off the field.

Playing for Beddau was a fantastic learning experience. Beddau and Senghenydd were probably the best two sides in the mid-district area at the time, but there were several other good sides in south and west Wales that we got to play. Similarly to Taff's Well, Beddau had some decent players and a few comedians in their ranks, players who were dedicated to the club but also wanted to have fun with it. In the season I joined, 1972-73, we played some excellent rugby and achieved some good results against some very respectable opposition.

It wasn't just the players who stood out at Beddau RFC. Everywhere in the set up were great people. You had Walford and Kath, who were the life and soul of the rugby club as its steward and stewardess. Then there was the dynamic trio of Glenog the physio, 'Porky' Harrison the linesman, as well as Terry Lloyd, a fantastic personality who ran the rugby club with his enthusiasm and leadership.

Glenog was a legend in his own right. He was a big man with a handlebar moustache, and always carried a photo of himself with his arms aloft in a classic boxing pose. It's said that a little knowledge can be a dangerous thing, and Glenog, in his role as physio, was extremely dangerous with his only injury apparatus being a bucket of cold water and a sponge – ideal for boxing but not so much for rugby injuries.

On one occasion, when Beddau were playing Llanelli Wanderers at Stradey Park, with my brother, Chris, playing at flanker, he received a nasty blow to the face, and immediately put his hands over his nose, which was in a real mess, clearly broken and disjointedly pointing to the side of his face. Quick as a shot, Glenog ran onto the pitch armed with his sponge and bucket of water. Of course, being an ex-boxer, Glenog considered a broken nose a mere hindrance. My brother's eyes were streaming, and he was in tremendous pain, but by the time Glenog had finished with him, he was going to be in a lot more pain. Standing face-to-face with my brother Glenog raised his hands to Chris' face and clapped his hands together trying to force the nose back into position. I swear Chris left the ground by a good five feet and, almost before he landed, Glenog had signalled to the referee that Chris was ready to play on! My brother returned to the fray with his nose looking distinctly red, throbbing and obviously incredibly painful. I think he was was expecting a visit to a local hospital rather than Glenog's emergency surgery.

I also once suffered from Glenog's healing hands. Beddau were playing in Aberdare on a wet day on a boggy pitch in the middle of winter, and both teams were slugging it out. I had received a blow on my ankle earlier in the game, and the pain was getting worse, especially as I was taking all the kicks. I eventually went down in some pain, and it was so bad I couldn't escape the attentions of our slowly advancing first-aid guru. "What's the matter, Taff," he asked (everyone was known as Taff by Glenog). I told him that I thought I had severely injured my ankle. After applying the freezing cold water inside my left boot, his expert opinion was that it was something muscular and that the remedy was to stamp my foot as hard as I could into the ground and the pain would probably go away. Thanks, Glenog, I thought.

However, towards the end of the game, I had to go off as my ankle was now really painful. When I got to the changing rooms, they had to cut my boot off because the swelling was so bad I couldn't get my foot out of the boot. I was taken to the local hospital, where they confirmed, to no-one's surprise, that I had broken my ankle and had been playing for over an hour in this state. Good work, Glenog!

Glenog and his antics are the stuff of rugby legend, but when combined with his partner in crime, Terry Lloyd, the dynamic duo created absolute mayhem.

Glenog had many other 'skills' apart from being a physio, one being his powerful singing voice, and he wasn't shy to break into song at a moment's notice. Terry loved to give Glenog different dares and to put him forward for competitions against anyone who also fancied a bizarre challenge. One night, after the club dinner, which started at Beddau clubhouse at 7pm on Saturday and ended at approximately 5pm on Sunday afternoon in Trefforest, Terry had wagered that Glenog could go up three flights of stairs and sing from the attic, and that he could be heard in the bar in the club as clear as a bell. Up the stairs went the gentle giant (he was around six foot four inches tall and weighed about 18 stone) and surely enough, upon reaching the attic, he started singing, really going for it at full volume. Downstairs in the bar, the noise was deafening.

Glenog came back down the stairs, and when he entered the bar, looking rather proud of himself, he asked Terry, "How was that, Taff?" Keeping a perfectly straight face, Terry replied "I didn't know you had started." With that, Glenog stormed back up the steps to have another go, to really bring the house down, and he nearly did! When he returned to the bar again, none of us could contain ourselves. We all fell about laughing, telling our confused and exhausted physio that there may have been some vague sounds coming from the attic.

The other challenge Terry set Glenog was for him to take on all-comers in a cheese-eating competition. The contest was to eat four pounds of cheese as quick as you could, with the winner taking all the money that was gambled. I never did see anyone beat Glenog. The fact is not many tried after seeing the state of him after eating four pounds of cheese!

No collection of rugby anecdotes is complete without an experience in Paris, and Glenog delivers perfectly. Glenog and several other Beddau RFC lads had travelled to watch Wales play France, and the boys decided to have a quick drink in a small bar in Paris. Everything was going well until Glenog went outside and suddenly there was a massive screech of brakes and the sound of breaking glass. A startled Parisian ran into the bar and muttered something about "*L'astronaute Gallois*" ("the Welsh astronaut"). Glenog had tried to cross the road but had looked left instead of right! The car had no chance, it hit Glenog skywards, and he landed on the bonnet, with his head smashing the car windscreen. Terry went with Glenog to the local hospital where, luckily, the medics said he was not critically injured, but was very disorientated and picking bits of glass from his forehead. Terry had a quick word with the hospital staff and informed Glenog that it would cost him 120 francs a night to stay in the hospital. As quick as a flash, Glenog instructed Terry to get his clothes out of the locker by the bed, and they were soon on the way back to the delights of Paris, to meet up with the rest of the Beddau RFC boys on tour!

Bryn 'Porky' Harrison, was another massive character. He was the club's linesman (the two competing clubs always provided a linesman each), and let's just say he had 'moments of bias' in our favour. During one game against Rhymney, their winger broke away on the halfway line and ran the ball in under our posts. It was a superb solo effort. As the Rhymney players were celebrating, it was brought to the referee's attention that Porky, standing on the halfway line, had his flag up. According to Porky the winger had stepped into touch. From my position the winger was a good three yards in from the touchline but Porky was adamant, and his deadpan expression left the referee with no choice but to disallow the try.

I think his finest performance was in the Welsh Cup game away to Tumble RFC, who had remained unbeaten at their own ground for two years. They were captained by Alun John, the brother of the great Barry John, and also fielded another John brother, Clive. It was an extremely close game that went down to the wire. Porky, with his debateable calls, had been on top form for us that day and, during the second half, the game stopped for a lineout on the Tumble supporters' side of the pitch. Just as the lineout was to be taken, we noticed Porky had disappeared. The Tumble supporters had finally had enough of his dodgy decisions, and had dragged him into the crowd. They were giving him a 'right going over'. It was the only time in my rugby career that I heard a referee say, "If I don't get my linesman back immediately, I will cancel the game", and I think he was serious too!

The battered touch judge emerged from the crowd and the game restarted. We were losing as we headed into final few minutes but I managed a last-gasp drop goal to give us a 21-20 victory. As the referee blew the final whistle the home crowd ran onto the pitch to, I stupidly thought, congratulate us on our victory, but they had other things on their mind and were determined to give our whole team a good going over as well. I soon felt the strength of feeling from one Tumble RFC supporter who bent his umbrella over my head. To cap it all, we were requested to leave the Tumble clubhouse by the club's officials as soon as we'd showered and clothed. Porky had given us the benefit of his line-calls but the home crowd had seen right through him.

Club Secretary Terry Lloyd's speciality was, after the game, to sabotage the drinks of the referee. Terry had it down to a fine art, asking the poor referee what he wanted to drink and then proceeding to make a cocktail of his own. It was not unusual to see the referee of the day staggering out of the clubhouse and many a time, a friend or a relative had to be called to come to the rescue of an unfortunate official.

William Gerald Jones, or 'Bones' as he was known by everyone in our rugby circles, was the tight-head prop for Beddau. He was an excellent player and yet another comedian. Once we were playing Brecon in the Welsh Cup, and it was our luck to have Ernie Lewis as the referee. Only that morning Ernie had been dropped from the international panel of referees so he was not in the best of moods. Before the game he got both sets of players to fill in every tiny hole on the rugby pitch with sand. His attitude became even worse when Bones decided to play the fool early in the game.

As the front rows went down for a scrum there was an almighty scream and the scrum collapsed. It sounded like someone had been seriously injured underneath the pile of bodies. You can imagine Ernie's face when he discovered it was a false alarm. Bones had spotted an Embassy 6 cigarette card in the mud as the scrum engaged and as an ardent collector of cigarette cards, he feared it might be trampled into the ground by the two packs of forwards. "What's the problem?"

asked Ernie. "Just a number six coupon, I collect them you see", said Bones. A lot of decisions went Brecon's way after that. On this of all days, that Saturday was not the day to mess Ernie Lewis about.

Ray Shearan, was Beddau's outside-half and was an extremely talented player who could easily have gone on to play for one of the top clubs in Wales. That didn't appeal to Ray, though, who preferred to stay in his village enjoy his rugby and have a few beers with the rest of his mates, particularly on a Friday night which would typically be a heavy session. As the outside-half, Ray would call all the moves for the centres and I would relay the calls to the backs outside me. Once we were playing Rhymney RFC at home and had a lineout very early in the game, 40 yards out from the Rhymney line. It was the first opportunity for the backs to have a set move, so I shouted to Ray to find out what the call was so I could let the other players know. When he answered me, it came out as complete gibberish, it sounded something like "forgssth". When I asked him to repeat it, his reply was equally incomprehensible and by now the backs outside me, eager to get stuck in and show what they could do, were getting a little bit annoyed with Ray and myself.

This non-communication continued throughout the first half, much to our puzzlement and frustration, and it was only when we got to half-time that we discovered what the problem was. Ray had been drinking all Friday night and was very much feeling the effects of that heavy session. Even worse than that, his speech was impaired because, after staggering home and finally managing to get the key in the lock, Ray had fallen through the doorway and as he hit the floor his top set of false teeth flew out of his mouth and was picked up by Clyde, his bull-terrier, who swallowed them whole. Without his teeth, Ray's on-field calls had made no sense at all! Our half-time team talk became a fiasco as we all fell about laughing while hearing him tell his story. The opposition must have heard us through the wall and wondered why we were all in hysterics!

We had a good side at Beddau; we won the Mid-District Cup and won a large number of games. We had a good run in the Welsh Cup, beating Glamorgan Wanderers, before beating a good Tumble side, thanks in part to Porky. In the next round we were drawn against Neath at home, and we were quietly confident of an upset at our place. It was a huge and very lucrative fixture, and we were all looking forward to the game. Unbelievably, Neath refused to play the game in Beddau, and the WRU moved the game to Penygraig, on a Wednesday night! Can you imagine that now, a team refusing to play, not for health and safety reasons, just because they didn't want to!

To make matters worse, I missed the game. I was still living in London as a student, so it was arranged that one of the local Beddau lorry drivers picked me up in London, and take me to Penygraig. It was a massive occasion for me and the club, so you can imagine my disappointment when, due to the traffic caused by everyone travelling to the Rhondda village for the game, I missed the kick-off by five minutes and I was the team's goal-kicker. Kenny Cooper had been quickly slotted in to take my place, but in all fairness to Kenny when he saw me on the side of the pitch, he offered to come off so I could play, but that just did not seem right or fair. My brother Chris, who also played that day, later told me that during the first lineout, the Neath prop, the notorious Walter Williams, took the trouble to ask all the Beddau forwards, "Who's your hard man then?" He was a fearsome sight, and all the boys in our pack pointed in all different directions bar pointing at themselves! We lost the game 12-6. Neath then lost the semi-final to Llanelli, who went on to beat Cardiff in the final and win the Cup in 1973. Missing that quarter-final, to the then reigning Welsh Cup holders (Neath had won the inaugural Cup in 1972), was gutting. I really wanted to test myself against the best in Wales, so to miss that opportunity due to traffic was a real frustration.

During my time with Beddau I had received offers to play for Cardiff, Newbridge and Bridgend, so I had a difficult decision to make at the end of the season. I was now 22 and felt ready to move up to first-class rugby. Cardiff was a club I admired, and I was attracted to play there. However, when I looked at their side, they had established internationals in their ranks, and I was not sure if I could become a regular player, so that was a bit daunting. I was desperate to play at the top level of Welsh club rugby, and knew that without the chance of playing week-in week-out, I would never reach my goal of pulling on the red Welsh jersey.

Near the end of the season, with thoughts of the offers from other clubs swirling around my head, Aberavon invited me to play for them against Pontypridd, at Ynysangharad Park. Also asked to play was a winger called Ffrangcon Owen, from Tonyrefail, who I would link up again with at Bridgend with significant effect. I could not believe that I was playing in such a high profile game between two of the biggest clubs in Welsh rugby. Unfortunately for me, Aberavon's outside-half Dai Prenderville clearly had no confidence in passing the ball outside him to the young, raw centre or the new winger. Dai had been on Llanelli's books but had found his way into the side blocked by a certain Phil Bennett, so was now trying his luck at Aberavon. Dai spent the game kicking away any possession we won, or calling set moves involving a miss-pass and a decoy runner, which was always me. It quickly became quite apparent that playing in the game was a waste of time. The best example of this was when Dennis John, the Pontypridd scrum half, dropped a goal from the back of a scrum near the halfway line to put Pontypridd 6-3 up. Dai Prenderville inexplicably asked me why I had not charged the kick down! How could it be my fault? I was 30 yards away standing in my position in the centre, when he dropped the goal, and I was to blame for what proved to be the final result!

It was so disappointing not to have been given a chance to show what I could do with the ball in hand, but that wasn't the end of a bad night. In those days players were given 'beer tokens' – for five free pints each after the game – and it was the captain's responsibility to hand them out to his players. Aberavon's captain was Iain Owen and as he was moving around the bar handing out the tokens to the Aberavon players, he took one look at me, and either thought I would not be playing for them again or did not recognise me as someone who had played that night for Aberavon because he completely missed me out! That was the final straw for me. I'd had no passes all night, I'd been blamed for Aberavon losing and now no free beer! Luckily for me, Ponty stalwart Bob Penberthy, who played over 800 games for the club, saw the beer incident and came across to speak to me. "Here Steve, have my beer cheques, I'll get some more off the Pontypridd committee members." A grand gesture from a great man. Bob also went onto say, "Don't play for that bunch of bastards, come and play for us at Pontypridd."

The final insult that day at Ynysangharad Park came when the Aberavon chairman, who was on the WRU selector's committee, asked me if I wanted to play the following week against Northampton RFC at Franklin Gardens? My response was short and precise, "You must be fucking joking!" That was the only time I ever played for a first-class team in rugby union other than Bridgend.

During my time playing for Beddau, I also had the strange experience of playing alongside my brother, Chris, against my other brother, Mark, who played centre for Senghenydd, which had been our father's club for many years. Mark was a good player and went on to play for Newport. The close proximity of decent and passionate village teams, and the rivalry they engender, were and still are to a great extent the hallmark of Welsh club rugby.

I had a fantastic time in my short period with Beddau RFC, but I ultimately followed in the footsteps of club legend, flanker Gary Prothero, who left Beddau for Bridgend RFC, was capped for Wales (11 times) and became a British and Irish Lion (in 1966). The larger 'elite' clubs only succeeded because of the players produced at grassroots, community clubs like Taff's Well RFC and Beddau RFC. Playing at that level taught me so much and I'm thankful to them both. I have great memories of my time playing in the green and gold of Beddau RFC – a brilliant club – but it was time to move on.

6

Bridgend RFC 1973-77

'I had the pleasure of playing with Steve, as the centre partnership for Bridgend, well over 100 times. He was never ruffled, never panicked and never lost his cool. Steve was great to play alongside and great off the field too – so laid back and no histrionics – and grateful for any favours that came his way. If you had to choose people to go into the jungle with he'd be top of the list. An all-round Top Man!'
Lyndon Thomas (Bridgend RFC and Wales 'B')

Thanks to Ivor John, a member of the Bridgend RFC committee who invited me to guest for them against Swansea RFC at the Brewery Field, I began a long and successful relationship with the club. I'd received offers from other clubs including Cardiff, where I thought I'd be used as a bench-warmer, and Newbridge, against whom I'd played well in the Welsh Cup but who were too far to travel to regularly, but at Bridgend I was welcomed into the side and instantly made to feel at home, even though I was taking someone's spot in the team at centre. If I remember rightly, Swansea beat us 13-9 but, from a selfish point of view I had a good debut, kicking all nine points. The ground was packed, but at my first game a wag in the crowd shouted, "Oi Fenwick! If they've got anymore like you up in Beddau, send them down here!"

I liked what I saw and joined the club in time for the start of the 1973-74 season. It was the beginning of a wonderful relationship with Bridgend RFC and I really appreciated the support I received from Lyndon Thomas, an established centre at the club, who had a major influence on my career both on and off the field. As per usual, when a new player comes into the squad there is more competition for that position but Lyndon, who featured in the midfield along with Norman Lang and outside half Ian Lewis, and who could have seen my arrival as a threat, couldn't have done any more to help me. Considering that Lyndon was, at that time, a Wales 'B' international and could have been excused for focussing fully on himself and his quest for a full Wales cap, the fact that he helped me as he did shows the type of man he is.

His support extended off the field as he also helped me out transport-wise. At the time, as I could still not drive, I had to travel from my home in Groeswen to Caerphilly, and then catch a bus to Cardiff where Lyndon would pick me from outside Thomson House, the former *Western Mail* office in the centre of Cardiff, and take me to the Brewery Field. To get home, I had to walk to the train station in Bridgend, catch a train to Cardiff, then a bus to Caerphilly and walk back the couple of miles to Groeswen. Looking back, it would have made far more sense for me to have signed for either Pontypridd or Cardiff, both being just a few miles away.

I'd plumped for Bridgend, however, so accepted the awkward travelling arrangements, and with the help of Wendy and Bryn, her father, as well as Lyndon, I made the trip to the Brewery Field three or four times a week. We usually had training on a Monday, a game on a Wednesday, Thursday was training and then another match on a Saturday. As my international rugby career took off I also had Wales squad training at Aberavon on Sundays. The constant round of buses, lifts, and walking miles after training finally spurred me to start driving lessons and it was such a relief to pass my test in Pontypridd. At last I could take full responsibility for my travelling requirements which made things so much easier all-round, for me and my list of 'taxi drivers'.

My first season with Bridgend went very well. We played 51 times, winning 38, losing 11 and drawing two. I played regularly and scored 230 points as Bridgend finished third in the Merit Table, the unofficial Welsh Championship. Bridgend had been very welcoming and had instantly made me feel at home, which was a strong factor for me to join them, but another key element was their style of play. Bridgend played attractive, attacking 15-man rugby, and that was exactly how I wanted to play the game.

44

With that playing philosophy, it is no surprise that we were a real force in sevens rugby and when competing in the popular tournaments at the time, such as the Snelling Sevens, the Welsh National Sevens and the Ayr Sevens in Scotland. Our team at Bridgend overflowed with pure rugby talent that suited the 7-a-side game perfectly, such as Viv Jenkins, who in my opinion, was the unluckiest player never to win a Welsh cap. He was a fabulous player who could unlock any team's defence but, unfortunately for him, his career dovetailed with some great Welsh wingers such as Gerald Davies and JJ Williams. He was some player, though. Other Bridgend players who shone on the sevens stage were Ian Lewis, Gerald Williams, Alan Walters, Meredydd James, Geoff Davies, Billy Pole, Phil Martell, John Lloyd, Gareth Williams and Ffrangcon Owen. All very gifted players.

We weren't just blessed with talented players, our coach Leighton Davies was pretty special too. He would analyse your game and give an honest opinion on your performance, and he wasn't afraid to knock you down a peg or two if he felt it was required. He was a great influence on me. There would be games where I had scored a lot of points and was feeling good about myself, but Leighton would bring me back down to earth with a bump by reminding me of a couple of missed kicks at goal or a poorly directed kick that almost resulted in a try for the opposition. In terms of accolades, if Leighton said you had a good game, then that was high praise indeed. As a young player you didn't get carried away, and knew hard work was required to reach the goal of playing for Wales. I don't think I could have been in a better playing and coaching environment.

It became quickly apparent that I had to get more pace into my game if I wanted to become a top player at this level, so I decided that in addition to the training I was doing with Bridgend, I would develop my running speed by pounding the road by Castell Coch in Tongwynlais for an hour every night when I didn't have other committments. In all honesty, I think it only made a tiny improvement on my pace, but it gave me the self-belief that I had the speed and stamina to outpace opposition players when needed.

The Bridgend team was very fit thanks to Leighton who demanded that we became one of the fittest teams around in order to play our 15-man rugby. He was a certainly a hard taskmaster, like on the evening when pitch was unavailable to us because of bad weather. We stupidly thought we might get a night off, but Leighton arranged a training routine in the main stand at the Brewery Field which involved us running up and down the stairs and doing various exercises at given points in the session. It was probably one of the hardest and most painful sessions I ever took part in. After that I prayed for good weather conditions for all training sessions.

One game that stood out during that first season was a game against Cardiff at the Arms Park. We had a bit of a jinx over Cardiff and over my Bridgend career we had an excellent record against them. The Cardiff side that season included surperb players such as Gareth Edwards, Gerald Davies, Alex Finlayson, PL Jones, Ian Robinson and Mike Knill, many of whom were full internationals. I lined up opposite Alex Finlayson, who was in the Wales squad at the time. The *Western Mail* headline that day read, 'Finlayson back off a skiing holiday for Bridgend game'. I had a good game but Alex was having a hard time of it. Crowds at rugby games can be a fickle lot, to say the least and at one line out, and loud enough for the whole crowd to hear, a frustrated Cardiff fan shouted, at his own player, "Why don't you fuck off back to your ski-ing holiday for another week!" Finlayson's confidence must have taken a huge dent. In contrast, a well-known Bridgend supporter came up to me at the end of the match to say, "You've earned yourself a bonnet [cap] after that performance." That was all the encouragement I needed. I'd out-played a member of the Wales squad and felt I was surely on my way to international selection. We pulled off the victory and clinched the double over Cardiff that season.

I also recall playing Cardiff years later when, just before we came out to play, it was announced over the tannoy that Gareth Edwards would not be playing and that a certain Terry Holmes would be replacing him. Gareth liked to manage his game time with Cardiff and I know our scrum half Alan Walters really enjoyed giving him some sledging when they played against each other. We all thought that with no Gareth and someone called Holmes playing, who had only just broken into their side, this change would significantly improved our chances of winning. Terry, however, had an outstanding game, giving our back row real challenges throughout, and we all came off the Arms Park pitch knowing full well who Terry Holmes was.

I'd been playing well and the Welsh media had been commenting that an international call up may not be too far away for me. With the

BRIDGEND RFC 1973-77

Probables v Possibles 'trial' game at Cardiff Arms Park on the horizon, I did wonder if I would be considered for selection but, once again, Leighton made sure I was not losing focus. During a training session, and in front of the Bridgend team, he said, "Hey Steve, if you keep playing as you are you may even get a trial, you never know". It was a great boost but also a reminder that I needed to maintain high standards.

Fortunately for me, I was selected for the trial game and it was the first time I came across the great Ray Gravell, the Llanelli centre. He would become my centre partner for Wales for many years and a huge influence on me. On that occasion I was not selected to play for Wales after the trial, but I knew that I was now on the selectors' radar so I just had to keep working on my game. Leighton kept my feet on the ground, and helped me improve my game. He was usually correct with all his observations on my general play and contribution to the team around the field.

The following season, 1974-75, truly set me on my international career. Captained by Derek Brain, a fine back-rower and a great guy, we finished seventh in the Merit Table, after playing 53 games in all competitions, winning 36, losing 16 and drawing one.

It was a big season for our prop forward, Brian Jones, a farmer from Llantwit Major, who clocked up his 550th appearance for the club. Brian is an incredible character who still calls me 'Frank', as do a few of my former teammates. The name comes from a infamous programme for a game between Bridgend and Bristol. One can only imagine that the secretaries from the respective clubs were discussing the team line-ups over a bad telephone line because several players took on whole new personas in the printed programme. It was hilarious. I became Frank Stenwick, while our hooker, Kerry Townley, was listed as Jeremy Chumley, among many other howlers. We were in stitches while reading the programme before the game, and the name stuck. I became Frank.

Towards the end of the season, in April 1975, Bridgend RFC travelled to the USA for a tournament in Santa Monica, California. An overseas rugby tour is always a highlight, and this one was no different. The competition consisted of teams from New Zealand, France and Canada, with us and Abertillery flying the flag for Wales. The tournament lasted ten days and we played well and won, but it was the off-field antics that stick in my mind, and three stories in particular, with Ian Stephens, Alan Walters and me playing starring roles.

DRAGONS AND LIONS

Like me, Ian 'Ike' Stephens also started his rugby career with Taff's Well RFC and has been a great friend over the years. His wife, Jackie, and my wife, Wendy, are great friends and we have spent a lot of time together. Ian started off as a lock forward, but after joining Bridgend, Leighton Davies and John Lloyd put him in the front row. It was a masterstroke as he went on to play for Wales and the British and Irish Lions with great distinction.

Ian has always had a great turn of phrase to cover all aspects of the English language and is a very entertaining person. During the tournament, a large group of players visited Hollywood where we, surprise surprise, ended up in a bar. where the bar staff seemed to be ignoring us. Unable to attract their attention, and gasping for a drink, there were 32 of us lined up waiting to buy a pint each when the manager suggested we should give the bar staff a tip for their trouble as a way to quicken the pace. The bar manager's face was a picture, thinking a tip from all the 32 lads was about to come her way. Her attitude didn't go done well with the boys, particularly Ike, and after pouring all the beers herself, he gave her a tip she didn't see coming: "Don't wash your face with broken glass," he said as he walked away. Needless to say, we had to go somewhere else for another pint!

Alan Walters, who played scrum-half, was another character in the group. On our way to San Francisco, we decided to stay overnight in Bakersfield and carry on the journey to San Francisco the following day. Bakersfield is a small place and there didn't seem to be much going on. Once again, 32 of us decided to have a few beers before bedtime. Alan, or 'Wally' as he is known, was in charge of the beer kitty. Wally is a chirpy character, and he led us into the nearest bar where he raced up to the bar to get the drinks flowing.

All of a sudden the whole place went quiet and it dawned on the rest of us that we were the bar's only white customers. On top of that the pool table was covered in playing cards and hundreds of dollars. Focusing on his kitty-man duties and totally unaware of the situation, the silence was broken by Wally who asked the barman for "32 pints of beer please, butt".

The barman, still stunned by these 32 hefty boys from 'out of town' turning up at the bar asked, "Where are you guys from?" "Wales, mun," Wally replied. "Oh, England," said the barman. "No, Wales, mun! Where Tom Jones is from." "Oh," said the barman, sounding relieved, before turning to the other patrons in the bar to say, "These guys are from Wales, where Tom Jones is from." The atmosphere in the bar instantly changed for the better! The barman proceeded to tell us that he and his regulars had gone silent in shock when we'd first walked into the bar because, in 30 years since the bar had opened, not one white person had set foot in there! Then Wally from Wales comes in with 31 others!

Once in San Francisco we wanted to go sightseeing and the plan was to visit Alcatraz Prison. Unfortunately, the weather was terrible with torrential rain which meant we defaulted to type and went to the nearest bar instead where someone had the bright idea to drink rounds of cocktails. We had no idea what we were doing and started downing the drinks as if they were going out of fashion. As the afternoon went on, the boys' heads began to drop as they fell asleep one-by-one. We had been well and truly introduced to Harvey Wallbangers.

While others were falling by the wayside I had the sense to leave the bar and catch a tram back to the hotel for a sleep, but the Wallbangers had clearly kicked-in. As I ran to catch a tram that was heading up one of those steep San Francisio hills it felt like I was running in slow motion. I just couldn't generate enough speed. I finally managed to grab hold of the back of the tram but couldn't lift my feet onto its steps. The passengers feared I could fall off so held my arms and I was now hanging off the back of the tram, being dragged up the hill, all the way back to my hotel. It was like a scene from a Buster Keaton film. As the tram came to a stop near to my hotel I managed to stand up and thank the other passengers for their help as I tried to regain some semblance of dignity. Looking down, I saw that a nice pair of shoes had been turned into a pair of sandals with bits of leather and sole scattered across the road behind me!

In addition to playing for Bridgend I was selected for what was initially classed as a Wales 'B' fixture against Tonga at Penygraig. I played alongside Ray Gravell and we clicked instantly. Ray was a rock in defence – 'Ray Gravell Eats Soft Centres' read the famous banner in a 1970s Gren cartoon – and was a real team player. "If one gets past you, I'll take him," said Grav before our first game together, "and if one gets past me, you'll take him. No one will get past the two of us." He was a dream to play with and from that very first game, we just clicked. For such an uncompromising player Ray suffered terribly from self-doubt and constantly needed reassurance. I remember playing against Llanelli when he totally flattened me with a massive, typically Grav, hit. Within seconds he was at my side as I lay in the mud. "You alright Steve?" he asked. "I hope I haven't hurt you." That was Grav. What a lovely man.

We won the game 26-7 and I managed to score a try. It was the start of 20 games together in the centre with Wales over six years and I believe ours was a partnership that served Wales well. Years later that game was reclassified as a full international but, for me, I still class my first international cap as the game against France the following year.

For the 1975-76 season, my good friend Lyndon Thomas was made Bridgend captain, an honour he fully deserved. Again, we played well as a team, finishing fifth in the Welsh Merit Table, playing 53 times, winning 35, losing 15 and drawing three. Our leading scorer was outside-half Ian Lewis, who scored 284 points, breaking the 279 points club record held by Keith Bradshaw set in the 1964-65 season. Ian was a very skilful player and another who was unlucky not to have been capped by Wales, but there were many talented Welsh outside halves playing at that time such as Phil Bennett, John Bevan, Keith James, Dai Richards, Gareth Davies and Bernard Thomas. All superb players.

The following season, with Lyndon continuing as club captain, was pretty similar with 34 victories and 16 defeats in our 50 games. During that 1976-77 campaign Bridgend acquired the services of a certain JPR Williams from London Welsh, which was quite a coup, and helped us to raise our standard as a squad. In addition to our impressive 15-man performances, we won the Snelling Sevens and the WRU National Sevens, which emphasised our ability to shine at the seven-a-side format.

It was during this period that I experienced the two contrasting attitudes of my international teammates when I played against them at club level: those who wanted to help you and those who just wanted to injure you. I was selected to play for Glamorgan against Monmouthshire, in a game to be played on a wet, windy Monday night, a couple of days after a Wales international match, at Eugene Cross Park, Ebbw Vale. We had a decent side and I lined-up alongside my club captain, Lyndon Thomas. Monmouthshire boasted a strong team including a forward pack of seven internationals, the exception being Mel Bevan of Tredegar RFC who was a fine player in his own right, and our forwards got a right going over.

Top left: Mam and Dad - Jack and Margaret Fenwick.
Top middle: Aged nine, at Aunty Rose's house in Dyffryn Ffrwd, Nantgarw.
Top right: The 14-year-old Caerphilly Grammar School pupil.
Right: Aged 18, with Chris and our dog, Tina.
Bottom: The Fenwick Family - Jack, Chris, Mam, Mark, Me and Anne.

Above: Fynnon Taf (Taff's Well) Junior School 1ˢᵗ XV, 1960-61. I'm middle row, fourth from right.
Below: In 1961-62 our 7-a-side team won the Del Harries Memorial Cup. I'm front row, centre, holding the ball.

Above: Caerphilly Grammar School under-13s, 1963-64. I'm seated, third from right.
Below: With Taff's Well RFC youth team - winners of the Pontyclun Youth 7s in 1970.

On Tour in Cornwall with my teammates from Borough Road College, Easter 1970.

A constant in my life since our schooldays, and since we were married, Wendy has believed in me and supported me every step of the way, including as my in-house taxi driver to training sessions!

I enjoyed my time as a teacher at St. Cennydd School in Caerphilly, and when news broke of my selection for Wales in 1975, the pupils joined in the celebrations.

Above: My Wales debut, against *Les Bleus*, in 1975. My international career couldn't have started better, with a try and a rare win in Paris. Below: The programme notes for my first home game, against England.

S. P. FENWICK (Bridgend)

Centre. Born 7.7.51. 5 ft. 10 in., 13 st. Like Gravell, Steve Fenwick made his Welsh team debut against France this season and scored a try. He had played against France B before Christmas and with his strong running and powerful hand-off he brought plenty of impetus to the midfield attack. For his club he scored 230 points last season, mainly as an accurate goal kicker. Was a star for the lively village club Beddau before joining Bridgend last season. Strong tackler. P.E. teacher.

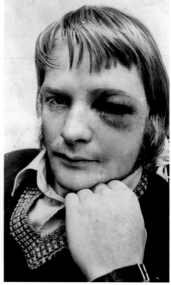

Above left: All smiles as I started my international career.
Above right: Nursing a painful black eye I received at Murrayfield on St. David's Day, 1975.

Right: Receiving
a pass from Grav,
Wales v Japan
(1975).

Below: Shopping
in Japan with (L-R)
Clive Rees, Roy
Bergiers, and Grav.

Below right: Wales v
Japan, Osaka.

Below: Lining-up for the anthems before playing Japan.

After a great time with Taff's Well RFC and Beddau RFC, I was invited to play for Bridgend RFC and spent seven wonderful years at the Brewery Field, winning the Welsh Cup twice and facing the All Blacks during our centenary year: (below, left) getting a friendly Llanelli *cwtch* from my friend Ray Gravell; (bottom, left), a quick word with JPR; (bottom, right) giving the Pontypridd players the eye after dislocating my shoulder in the 1979 Welsh Cup final; (below, right) a Grogg from my time with Bridgend RFC.

Touring was a key part of the game. For many of us it was the only opportunity we would have had to see the rest of the world. It was also such great fun, as seen here with Derek Quinnell (above left) and my Wales roommate Allan Martin (above right).

In action, supported by Ffrancon Owen, on tour in the US (1976).

With Gareth Davies, Brynmor Williams, Ray Gravell & Sandy Carmichael (Canada, 1976).

In Canada with the Baa Baas: (L-R) Dai Richards, Duncan Madsen, Mike Knill, Alan Tomes, and Andy Irvine.

The Mounties got their man, in Canada, 1976.

Above: In full flight, taking the battle to the English at Twickenham, 1976.

Kicking for territory, against France during the Grand Slam decider at the Arms Park, 1976. The two players behind my right shoulder need no introduction, but the player to my left, the Cardiff prop Mike Knill, won his one and only cap that memorable day.

My goal-kicking was getting noticed!

Above: Celebrating JPR's try against Ireland at the Arms Park, 1977.
Below: Perhaps the most important flick-pass of my career, to Phil
Bennett for 'that' try at Murrayfield in 1977. And, yes, I meant it!

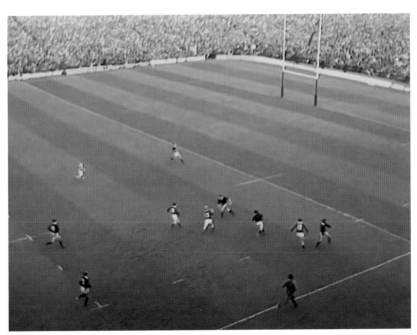

Two tries during the 1978 Grand Slam: (above) scoring in the corner against Scotland at the Arms Park against Scotland; (below) I scored 16 points against Ireland in Dublin, including this try, as we secured the Triple Crown to set up the Grand Slam decider against France.

Hoisting another kick, against Ireland at the Arms Park, 1979. We won, just, 24-21, to keep our hopes of another Championship title alive.

Caught by Peter Squires, against England in 1979, but we went on to win the game and secure the 'Quadruple Triple Crown', an amazing achievement.

I was honoured to have a number of Groggs made of me. John Hughes always expertly captured my ever-changing hairstyles and moustaches!

STEVE JOINS THE LEGENDS

By Jim Hill

STEVE FENWICK will equal the oldest international appearance record in world Rugby next week.

When he plays against England at Twickenham in eight days' time, Bridgend's brilliant British Lion will join legendary old-timer Arthur Gould as Wales's most capped centre.

A 25th cap for Fenwick is a mere formality which Wales's selectors will confirm when they announce the team for Twickenham today.

But it will bridge the longest gap left in the appearance record of any Rugby-playing nation in the world.

Fenwick will arrive at his record appearance exactly 83 years after the target was set by Newport's ancient threequarter star.

Gould played his Rugby in knickerbockers before the turn of the century, appearing a total of 27 times for Wales between 1885 and 1897—but playing twice at full-back.

Phelgmatic, unflappable Fenwick, 28-year-old joint managing director of an industrial cleaning firm, began his record run in 1975 and has played the last 22 games in succession.

The only one he has missed was in his first season. A fractured cheekbone against Scotland at Murrayfield kept him out of the next match against Ireland.

Fenwick is set for a record

BOB STOKOE

ROCHDALE 'REBELS' TACKLE

In 1979 I equalled the record for the most points scored in a Five Nations Championship, 38, and in 1980, against England, I broke Arthur Gould's 83-year-old record as Wales' most capped centre - another incredible achievement.

Due to my new commercial interests I declined the Lions tour to South Africa in 1980 and opted to captain the shorter Wales tour to North America. Not sure why Elgan Rees and I allowed the photographer to take this picture!

Appointed captain for the WRU's centenary season, 1980-81, it was a huge honour to lead my country during such an important period in the history of Welsh rugby.

The centenary year began with a match against an Overseas XV in September 1980, which we won and I scored a try (above). Next up were the All Blacks in early November (below, left) when we were easily beaten 23-3, before a combined Wales & England v Ireland & Scotland match in late November (below, right) which 'we' won. On the winning side in Cardiff - a novel experience for the England players!

Wales	New Zealand
Touch Judge: D. I. H. Burnett (I.R.F.U.)	Touch Judge: M. D.M. Rea d.R.F.U.)
Red Jerseys, White Shorts	Black Jerseys, Black Shorts
15 J. P. R. Williams	15 †D. L. Rollerson
Bridgend	Manawatu
14 H. E. Rees	14 S. S. Wilson
Neath	Wellington
13 D. S. Richards	13 B. J. Robertson
Bridgend	Counties
12 S. P. Fenwick (captain)	12 W. M. Osborne
Bridgend	Wanganui
11 †R. Ackerman	11 B. G. Fraser
Newport	Wellington
10 W. G. Davies	10 N. H. Allen
Cardiff	Counties
9 T. D. Holmes	9 D. S. Loveridge
Cardiff	Taranaki
1 C. Williams	1 †R. C. Ketels
Swansea	Counties
2 A. J. Phillips	2 H. R. Reid
Cardiff	Bay of Plenty
3 G. Price	3 G. A. Knight
Pontypool	Manawatu
4 D. L. Quinell	4 A. M. Haden
Llanelli	Auckland
5 G. A. D. Wheel	5 †G. Higginson
Swansea	Canterbury
6 P. Ringer	6 M. W. Shaw
Llanelli	Manawatu
8 †G. P. Williams	8 M. J. Mexted
Bridgend	Wellington
7 J. Squire	7 J. N. K. Mourie (captain)
Pontypool	Taranaki

When captain of the combined Wales and England team that faced Scotland and Ireland in 1980, I introduced the Queen to the players. My friendly quip, about the Welsh not normally getting along the English but having to grin and bear it that day, didn't go down well! I kept my mouth firmly shut when meeting Prince Charles.

Winning two Grand Slams and four Triple Crown from 1976 to 1979 was an outstanding achievement for Wales. It was also a great personal honour to be one of just seven players - alongside Geoff Wheel, Graham Price, Bobby Windsor, Allan Martin, JJ Williams & JPR Williams - to have been involved in every campaign.

It was a very physical game from the first whistle and our scrum-half had to go off injured after only ten minutes. Unfortunately, for me, we had no replacement in that position so Lyndon suggested that as I had played scrum-half as a youth I could fill in. Thanks, skipper! So, there I was, playing behind a pack getting destroyed, meaning I was going to get a pasting. Their forwards couldn't wait to give me a warm Monmouthshire valleys welcome I'd never forget. It was horrendous.

At one lineout, the Cardiff lock forward Phil Kallonas tapped the ball back in my general direction, leaving me to scramble on the floor desperately trying to get hold of the ball with the Monmouthshire pack charging straight at me. As I picked up the bouncing ball they descended on me and my Welsh teammate from two days previous, Graham Price, booted me straight in the guts. I was gasping for air and it is fair to say I was in a spot of bother. After I received treatment from the physio, I asked Pricey, "What the hell did you do that for?" To which he replied that if there was an opportunity to kick an opponent, and he didn't, Ray Prosser (the Pontypool coach) would drop him for the following week! Unbelievable!

The other, more caring side, came from a very surprising direction. Once, when we were playing Pontypool and there was an international game coming up that weekend, I was tackled and stuck at the bottom of a ruck. I just braced myself, waiting for the 'Viet Gwent' to run over me as they frequently did. Suddenly, Terry Cobner, the Pooler flanker and my Welsh teammate shouted, "Stay there". I had no option really, but Cobs laid over me, as his pack run over the top of us. After they'd gone he helped me up and said, "Now fuck off, you bastard". The one and only time playing against Pontypool when someone did something nice for me!

The 1977-78 season, under Lyndon's third successive campaign as captain, we played 50 games, winning 32, losing 16, and drawing two. Our scrum-half, Gerald Williams, had an outstanding season, scoring some crucial tries, while Gareth Williams, the back-rower, had a great season – including a call-up to the Wales 'B' squad – and was rightly named as the club's Player of the Year. Bridgend also retained the Snelling Sevens and the WRU National Sevens. We were a very good side that just needed a little bit extra to take us to the highest level of Welsh club rugby. The following year all that was to change.

7

Bridgend RFC 1978-81

'As a young boy from Pontycymmer, Bridgend were my team and Steve Fenwick was an idol. I admired the way he showed the deft touches, as he looked to play a teammate into space, but would have no qualms about getting stuck in a few minutes later. When I played rugby with my mates at Lawrence Park, home of Pontycymmer RFC, I was always Steve Fenwick, taking all the long-range match-winning kicks. I dreamt of one day emulating Steve by playing centre for Bridgend and Wales, but I never imagined that we'd both switch codes and play for our country in rugby league. There's a saying that we should never meet our idols as they'll only disappoint us. Whoever said that has clearly never met Steve Fenwick.'

John Devereux (Wales, British & Irish Lions, Wales RL, Great Britain RL)

Founded in 1878, the club, players and supporters all hoped our centenary season would bring the success we'd been so close to achieving. Bridgend were a thrilling side to watch and scored plenty of tries, but against the very best club sides, we just seemed to a lack a bit of grunt and power in the forwards, so the arrival of Billy Howe from local rivals Maesteg was a huge boost. Well respected by his peers, Billy was a hard-as-nails lock forward and recruiting him to the squad gave us the steel we needed.

BRIDGEND RFC 1978-81

Our captain for the centenary season was JPR Williams. The ultimate rugby player, he gave 100% in every game whether it was for club or country, and playing alongside him does not happen too often. His commitment to Bridgend was exemplified in 1977 when, after playing for Wales in the now classic game against Scotland at Murrayfield – during which he had been injured – he was back in action two days later as Bridgend faced Cross Keys. My lasting memory of that game is JPR having a wrestling match with Cross Keys' Glyn Bram, who loved a fight or two whenever he stepped on a rugby field. JPR never gave an inch, even just over 48 hours after playing an exhausting Five Nations match. He was the ultimate competitor, and to have him on your side was just so reassuring and gave you so much confidence. He would be my first choice as full-back in a World's Greatest XV.

During my centre partnership with Lyndon Thomas, we came up against some outstanding centre pairings and I always gave it my all regardless of the competition, but when you played against certain sides and looked at your direct opposition, you knew you were in for a tough game. In my time in union in Wales, I would say the three most difficult centre partnerships I came up against were Newport's Dai Burcher and Gareth Evans, Llanelli's Ray Gravell and Roy Bergiers, and Cardiff's Alex Finlayson and Mike Murphy. All but one of the six were Welsh internationals, and four were British and Irish Lions. When you add a number of other immensely talented individuals, like Dai Richards of Swansea and Ian Hall of Aberavon, the depth of incredibly gifted centres playing in Wales during that period is staggering. You could never let your standards slip, or your Welsh place would be gone, and it could be a long and tricky road to navigate to get the shirt back.

As we'd all hoped, Bridgend did indeed have an outstanding season in 1978-79, and JPR was magnificent, winning the club's Player of the Year award. We played 52 games, winning 42, losing 10 and finished runners-up to Pontypridd in the *Western Mail* Welsh Club Table. We finished third in the Whitbread Merit Table, behind Pontypridd and Maesteg, and also won awards from *Rugby World*, the *Daily Mail* and *Sunday Telegraph* for our performances.

The *Sunday Telegraph* award was based on the win to loss ratios for the clubs in England and Wales, and we came out on top with a win percentage of 83%. The top four, in order, were Bridgend, Pontypridd, Cardiff and Bath. It was a great achievement.

During the course of our centenary season, 45 players represented Bridgend, and there were some outstanding performances, such as winger Ian Davies who scored four tries against Penarth on his debut. Gareth Williams, the athletic back-rower, scored five tries against Penarth, which is a club record for a forward (he also scored four tries against the students of South Glamorgan Institute, Cyncoed). We played some great rugby and even managed to win the WRU's Schweppes Challenge Cup, after years of trying but never getting further than the semi-final.

In that cup run, we beat Abertillery, Newbridge, then Maesteg in the quarter-finals and Llanelli in the semi-finals. In the final we faced Pontypridd at Cardiff Arms Park. My good friend, and by then business partner, Tom David, captained Pontypridd but the Sardis Road side was led out that day by Bob Penberthy who was making his final appearance for the club after an astonishing 877 appearances. They were fired up and wanted to win it for the 'Bionic Elbow' as he was known. He was a fantastic servant to Welsh rugby.

It was a memorable game against a very good Pontypridd side. We were playing well and I was having a solid game having scored a try, kicked a conversation and also kicked three penalties. Disaster struck, however, in the first few minutes of the second half when I chased a kick and attempted to tackle Ian Walsh, the Pontypridd full-back who was looking to run the ball back. Ian tried to avoid contact and, in vain, I decided to ankle tap him. I didn't quite make it, just missed his legs and my outstretched arm seemed to get stuck in the grass, but my momentum was such that my body kept going. With my arm now stationary and my body in full flight something had to give. I felt a strange sensation in my shoulder, and it was clear that something had gone badly wrong.

I had dislocated my shoulder and had to leave the field to have the joint put back into its socket. It was a bizarre experience as the WRU doctor, a former hockey player called Gordon, who only had one eye, was smoking a cigarette while treating me. "Concentrate, Gordon!" I thought to myself as he took a drag on the fag while fumbling with my shoulder. Wendy, who had come to watch me play, was not too convinced the treatment was going as it should have and wanted me to go to the hospital to have it treated. However, good old Gordon succeeded in putting my shoulder back into place, and I watched the rest of the match from the sidelines as Bridgend won the game, and the cup, by beating Pontypridd 18-12. JPR lifted the trophy and I was awarded accolade of the Man of the Match, which was a pleasant surprise seeing that I left the game relatively early due to my injury.

As a result of the dislocated shoulder I was unable to drive for a few weeks, so my business partner, Tom David, who'd lined up against me at the Arms Park had the unenviable task of driving me around for all my work commitments. We had beaten Pontypridd in the final and now poor Tommy was forced to be my chauffer! As we travelled from meeting to meeting, with my arm in a sling, I lost no opportunity to remind our customers what had happened in the final, at Tom's expence but fair play to Tom, he took it on the chin. Sorry, Tom!

Winning the cup was the perfect end to our centenary year and our fantastic supporters thoroughly deserved it. For the record, the Bridgend team that day was: 15. JPR Williams; 14. Ian Davies; 13. Steve Fenwick (replaced by Chris Williams); 12. Lyndon Thomas; 11. Viv Jenkins; 10. Ian Lewis; 9. Gerald Williams; 1. Ian Stephens; 2. Geoff Davies; 3. Meredydd James; 4. Lyn Davies; 5. Roy Evans; 6. Gareth Jones; 8. Derek Brain; 7. Gareth Williams. Once the season ended, we went on a tour to Canada in May 1979, which was very successful and a great way to end that centenary season with a great group of lads.

Even though we won the cup, the highlight of the season for me was Bridgend being chosen to play the New Zealand All Blacks during their autumn tour. It was an incredible honour for the club and its supporters. The All Blacks deservedly won the game 17-6, but the encounter gained its place in sporting infamy when JPR Williams suffered a severe facial injury after being stamped on by All Blacks prop forward, John Ashworth. JPR left the field with his face covered in blood and a gaping hole in his cheek. Both JPR's father, Peter, and his brother, Chris (who replaced me in the WRU Cup Final), were medically qualified, as was JPR, and they managed to quickly stitch the wound.

He had lost two pints of blood and required 30 stitches in his face. That would normally be the end of the game and a visit to hospital for most players, but not for JPR. Ashworth's expression when he saw our full-back returning to the field of play a few minutes later was priceless. New Zealanders take no prisoners, though, and assuming he'd now be our weak-link they launched an up-and-under in JPR's direction to test his mettle. The All Black forward who charged at JPR thinking he'd be easy pickings soon discovered that our full-back was made of pure Welsh steel. After calmly catching the ball, JPR ran at and completely flattened the cocky Kiwi. The packed crowd roared its approval. What a player! We were in awe of him. He had our total respect.

Proving that our cup victory was no centenary year one-hit-wonder, we retained the Schweppes WRU Challenge Cup the following season, beating Swansea 15-9 in the final, with Ffrangcon Owen scoring a great try in the corner. Captained by my Welsh teammate, Geoff Wheel, Swansea were a good side and it was a tough encounter, but it was great to win the cup two years on the bounce with Meredydd James lifting the trophy. We seemed to have the knack of performing well in the cup and won through to the final the following season, a hat-trick of consecutive finals, but this time lost 14-6 to a fine Cardiff side.

At the end of that 1980-81 season, the team were to go on a summer tour but by then I knew I wouldn't just be leaving the club, but also rugby union, so I declined the offer to tour and told them to take a youngster instead of me who would benefit from the experience.

My time at Bridgend was brilliant. I loved the brand of rugby we played, and the players we had in the squad were such great characters on and off the field. It was a great mix, and all played their part. We had internationals such as JPR, Gerald Williams, Gareth Williams, Gary Pearce, Ian Stephens, and John Lloyd, as well as players who were never capped - unluckily in many cases. Meredydd James, Lyndon Thomas, John Morgan, Billy Howe, Geoff Davies, Brian Jones, Gary Williams, Ian Lewis, Gordon Collier, Derek Brain, Alan Walters, David Griffiths, and Viv Jenkins – to name just a few – were all superb rugby players, who contributed massively to that golden era.

It's a great club with great supporters and I owe them a huge debt of gratitude. I had many successful years which helped me launch my international career. Diolch, Bridgend RFC.

8

Wales 1975

'I vividly remember Steve's first appearance for Wales against France in Paris. His centre partner that day was my Llanelli teammate Ray Gravell, who was also making his Wales debut. Steve was a laid-back character, the exact opposite to Grav who was an emotional wreck and was having a job keeping it all together. In between the hysterical crying and punching holes in the changing room ceiling, Grav was belting out his favourite Dafydd Iwan songs while going back and forth to the toilet every two minutes. The Llanelli players were used to Grav's pre-match nerves but I remember the look of sheer disbelief on Steve's face as he calmly sat there, watching Grav. They had completely opposite temperaments but formed a perfect centre pairing and both played magnificently, enjoying the physical contact which the French did not always appreciate. Steve scored a try not long into the game and Wales came away with a great victory. That was the start of an outstanding Wales career for Steve Fenwick.'
Derek Quinnell (Wales, British & Irish Lions)

Following my solid game for Wales 'B' against Tonga, combined with my performance for Bridgend, I was catching the eye of the selectors, and I was chosen for the Wales team to play against France in Paris on 18 January 1975. It was a new-look side and I was one of six new caps alongside Pontypool's props, Charlie Faulkner and Graham Price, Llanelli's centre, Ray Gravell, Swansea's flanker, Trefor Evans and

Aberavon's outside-half, John Bevan. I had finally achieved my dream. All that hard work had paid off and my family were all very proud. I still get a buzz thinking of that moment.

It was an incredible feeling knowing I'd be playing alongside many of my Welsh rugby heroes such as Gareth Edwards, JPR Williams, Gerald Davies and Mervyn Davies. The players I'd supported at the Arms Park for the last ten years were now going to be my teammates. It was surreal.

We opened the 1975 Five Nations Championship campaign in Paris against a French side who were heavy favourites to win the game. It was a daunting task, and with six new caps we had been given very little chance of winning at the *Parc des Princes*. We got off to a great start and I scored a try after only five minutes. Not only that, Mervyn Davies, our inspirational captain, then asked me to take the conversion. I was shaking like a leaf, but I managed to put the ball between the posts. I remember thinking "I've got my Welsh cap and I've now scored a try for Wales. Nobody can ever take that away from me. Even if I'm never selected again, I've achieved my dream." Of course, that initial thought about being satisfied with a single cap soon disappeared as I simply couldn't get enough of playing for my country. I was hooked and never wanted it to end.

Much of the game was a blur but I do recall one incident when there was a break in play and I was catching my breath, still worried about the opponents I was facing. Grav and I, first cap novices in midfield against players such as Roland Bertranne and Claude Dourthe, feared what they could do with the ball if we gave them too much space. Suddenly, Roland shouted "Oi, Fenwick" and, once he'd got my attention, made a signal of a snake movement with his hand, taunting me he was going to get the ball and slide past me. I couldn't let that comment go and had to come back with a response, so I shouted back, "Me, a tank" and with my hands mimicked me driving a tank over his snake! I have no idea if he even understood. He must have thought I was a bloody idiot!

We put in an excellent performance and beat France 25-10, with tries from Terry Cobner, Gareth Edwards, Gerald Davies and Graham Price's iconic length-of-the-field effort to add to my early score. It may have been an experimental side but we were off the mark with an impressive away win. Having Mervyn Davies as captain, and former-

WALES 1975

Welsh international and British and Irish Lions star, John Dawes, as coach, I felt we were heading for an exciting period for Welsh rugby because they had similar views on how the game should be played. Both favoured a 15-man attacking style of rugby which was exciting for the supporters and also for the players. Little did I know how exciting and successful it was going to be.

That night at the official banquet I received my Welsh cap but after celebrating to, and past, the limit, I'd lost the cap by 8pm. Luckily, it was handed into the hotel we were staying at, and I breathed a huge sigh of relief. Great start, Fenwick!

The lasting memories I have of my Welsh debut are of exchanging shirts with Roland, who has remained a good friend over the years, and also when we were leaving the stadium by coach to return to the hotel in Paris and saw a huge crowd of French supporters who had gathered outside the ground. We feared they may be looking for some revenge for our victory, and we all braced ourselves for the worst. However, in true French rugby fashion, they had remained there to applaud us for the win and the way we had played. Fantastic memories I'll treasure forever. *Merci beaucoup, la belle France. Magnifique!*

Despite our victory in Paris, the strength of our squad meant I wasn't assuming I'd be automatically selected for the next game, against England, in Cardiff. In those days, and for a number of years after, players would discover their fate from the media, particularly via newspapers. If the headline on the hoarding outside the newsagent proclaimed something like 'New Caps Selected', you would panic, run in the shop and buy the paper to read whether that new cap was taking your place! Thankfully, I had kept my place in an unchanged team from the French win and I could not wait to step on to the hallowed Arms Park turf. The last time I'd played there was for Taff's Well under-11s, but now I'd be wearing the famous red Welsh shirt.

We won the game comfortably by 20-4, and I scored another try, as did wingers Gerald Davies and John James (JJ) Williams. Allan Martin, the lock forward who was a master of long-range place kicking, also got his name on the score-sheet with two penalty goals and a conversion. Captained by Fran Cotton, one hell of a character who remains a good friend, England crossed for a single Nigel Horton try. The English backs contained some excellent players such as David Duckham and Peter Squires, who was one of my best mates in rugby, and some outstanding forwards including Peter Wheeler (another good friend), Roger Uttley and Tony Neary.

After two wins in two games we headed to Murrayfield in confident mood. The game didn't go our way and, in front of what was at the time a world record attendance of a reported 104,000 people, Scotland managed to win the game 12-10. We lost by four penalties for Scotland, to one try – scored by Trefor Evans – and my two penalties, however, in addition to the enormous crowd, the game was memorable for me for a number of reasons.

After damaging a cheekbone in a collision, I was forced off the field and joined John Bevan, who had dislocated his shoulder earlier in the game, in the treatment room. Losing our outside half and centre disrupted our play somewhat, despite us being replaced by the talented Phil Bennett and Roger Blyth, who normally played full-back for Swansea. Our injuries were deemed serious enough for a visit to Edinburgh Royal Infirmary and so an ambulance was called to Murrayfield and the two of us settled down for the journey.

To our great surprise we were joined by an agitated Celtic supporter who was screaming in pain and frustration after injuring himself trying to climb the fence at Heart of Midlothian's nearby football ground, Tynecastle, to see his team play. If the screaming wasn't bad enough, the ambulance seemed to hit every bump and pot hole in the road as the three of us headed to hospital. The next few hours were unforgettable.

When we arrived at the hospital I honestly thought that as two of the patients were Welsh internationals, we would get some special treatment, like VIP's if you will. Unfortunately, this was not the case at all. John went off to one cubicle, and I went to another where the nurse told me to sit on a trolley, surrounded by curtains, and relax. I did as I was told but after a while it was obvious that there were no doctors around. After waiting a while longer I asked a nurse where the doctors were. "They're all watching the match on TV, she replied in a lovely Scottish accent. "Oh great", I thought. I'd had an excellent view of the game just 20 minutes earlier and now all I could see were cubicle curtains. To compound my growing discomfort, the nurse pushed her head back through those curtains and said, "You're losing 9-6". By then, sitting on a trolley in A & E with a damaged face and the swelling increasing by the minute, I didn't appreciate the running commentary.

WALES 1975

Finally, I was advised that Wales had lost 12-10, and that the doctors would be with me shortly. When they appeared and took a look at the mess that was my face, my worst fears had been confirmed – I had fractured my cheekbone. The knee of a Scottish forward who'd been running past me had made contact with my cheek as I was getting up off the floor. It was 40 yards away from the ball. An unfortunate accident?

The news was then broken to me that I'd have to stay the night in hospital but, as if it would really cheer me up, I'd be allowed a single can of lager as compensation for not attending the grand post-match dinner in Edinburgh. I did my best to thank the doctor for his attention, and then remarked that he looked very smart in his kilt and traditional Scottish outfit. "Yes," he said, "I'm going to the rugby dinner, the one you're missing".

Wendy, who'd been on a rugby trip to Edinburgh with friends, popped in to see me for a while, as did George Morgan, the WRU's Liaison Officer and a fellow school teacher in Caerphilly. Having checked how the two injured internationals were, he also rushed off to get ready for the rugby dinner. As you can imagine, I didn't take that well!

That night it felt like every drunk in Scotland had booked into the hospital for a warm night's sleep, and the noise kept me awake all night. It was unbearable. In the morning, when two doctors were discussing whether to keep me in Edinburgh or pass me onto Cardiff Royal Infirmary, I quickly interrupted to say in no uncertain terms that I was heading home with the team, then discharged myself and met up with the players and committee members and travelled back to Wales.

My home in Tongwynlais was close to the hospital in Cardiff, so on my return I arranged an appointment and my injury was treated, but I was definitely out of contention for the final match of the Championship. So was John Bevan.

Phil Bennett continued at outside half and his Llanelli teammate Roy Bergiers, an excellent centre, was called-up to replace me. They both played very well in a fabulous display by Wales, beating Ireland 32-4 at the Arms Park. Phil scored 12 points with his boot and Roy bagged one of our five tries, with Gerald Davies, Gareth Edwards, Charlie Faulkner and JJ Williams scoring the others. Roy's performance meant I was going to have to work and train even harder to get my place back in the Welsh team. Competition for selection, in every position, was so fierce that an untimely injury could mean you could be out for a considerable period. Welsh fans had an air of expectancy, as if they sensed something special was happening in Welsh rugby, and so it turned out to be.

Following that successful first season in the national squad, I was invited on my first tour with Wales, to Hong Kong and Japan in September 1975. The heat and humidity was new to us and it took a lot of getting used to, not least the excessive weight loss. Before the international against Japan in Osaka, the Welsh Physio Gerry Lewis gave us salt tablets to help maintain our hydration and I took loads, but still lost ten pounds! Following the game, two of the Japanese players were so dehydrated they collapsed on the pitch, and they were supposedly used to the heat!

The fact they were in such a state might have something to do with the Japanese players being outside far too early, well before the kick-off time, going through some rigorous warm up-exercises. Mervyn Davies, our captain, drew our attention to this excessive exercising going on while we were still sat, sweltering, in our changing room. Merv, smoking a cigarette while observing the Japanese players, said they "must be fucking mad" to warm-up like that in those conditions. He was right because they ran out of energy soon after half-time and we won the game 56-12.

Shiggy Konno, the manager of the Japan side, took the loss very badly and didn't allow any of his players to attend the after-match function. Socialising after a game is part of rugby culture and we were disappointed by his decision. His explanation was that they all had to work on Monday, although the perceived national humiliation was clearly the real reason, but after we expressed our disapproval and said how much we wanted to meet them, he changed his mind and the whole Japan team came to the post-match function. It was a lovely evening and we appreciated the opportunity to get to know our Japanese opponents.

It was a fascinating tour, and not just for rugby reasons as the second test was an even more emphatic 82-6 victory. It was a totally new culture, in terms of language, cusine and social norms, and so very different to what we were used to in Wales, and Europe in general. On one occasion Phil Bennett nearly caused an international incident when he decided to 'borrow' a bicycle to get back to our hotel after a function and was hotly pursued by a Japanese police patrol car. Luckily for Phil, the traffic was so heavy he had the edge on the police car and managed to reach the hotel and disappear before the police arrived.

We were well looked after, and with so many attractions and historical sites to visit we were never bored. We also got invited to a few Sumo wrestling bouts, which was fascinating. All the Sumo wrestlers spoke in an extremely squeaky voice caused by damaged vocal chords after taking blows to their throats by opposing wrestlers. It was very weird to hear a 28 stone ex-American footballer talk in such a high pitched voice. He informed us that the average life expectancy of a Sumo wrestler at that time was just 40 to 45 years of age, due to their excessive fighting weight and the strain it placed on their bodies. When the Sumo wrestlers were introduced to us, they could hardly believe that we were international rugby players, and fellow athletes, because we were at least half their size in stature and weight. Despite being treated like gods, I'm not convinced that the adulation was worth such a short life.

We returned from Japan and prepared for a huge match, against Australia in December 1975. Roy Bergiers had taken my place against Ireland and played so well in the game, scoring an excellent try, I half expected him to keep his position in the back line alongside his Llanelli teammates Phil Bennett, Ray Gravell and JJ Williams. The cheekbone was fixed, and I had played well for Bridgend since returning from the Far East, nevertheless, I was delighted, pleasantly surprised and very relieved to be back in the team so quickly. Roy displayed true sportsmanship as, despite being so disappointed, he was nothing but supportive – a true gentleman.

That wasn't always the case, particularly amongst the forwards. Around that time John Richardson and Mel Bevan were pushing Charlie Faulkner and Graham Price from the fabled Pontypool Front Row for starting slots and at a national training session at Aberavon I'm certain I overheard a plot being hatched by the 'Viet Gwent' to do some damage to John – along the lines of, "You hold him down and I'll kick his fucking head in" – to ensure Charlie kept his place. I also recall, as if it were yesterday, as the two mixed Welsh XVs lined up to face each other at training – there was no Probables v Possibles at training – when Terry Cobner shouted a warning so loud that the

5,000-plus crowd could easily hear. The Welsh captain Mervyn Davies had a habit of lying on the ball at rucks which obviously irked Cobner, who said, "If that long string of piss lies on the ball again, kick his fucking head in." That's pretty competitive just six days before a major game! The Pontypool guys were brutal. Terry Cobner was always good to me, mind, and I can remember a club game at Pontypool Park when I was caught at the bottom of a ruck and could hear the hooves of their pack charging at me. "Here we go," I thought. "No disco tonight back at the Brewery Field." Fearing the worst, Terry dived on top of me and protected me from the Pooler stampede. My Bridgend teammate Ikey Stephens wasn't so fortunate and found himself on the wrong end of some very large rugby boots.

John Bevan, who'd also been badly injured in Edinburgh earlier that year, was recalled to replace Phil Bennett who himself was injured. We easily beat Australia 28-3 in a great team display. JJ Williams, whose exceptional rugby ability was matched by his terrific pace that could destroy defences all around the world, scored a hat-trick of tries. Gareth Edwards also got in on the act, scoring his 18th try for Wales, which broke the Welsh try-scoring record of 17, jointly-held at that time by Johnny Williams, Reggie Gibbs and Ken Jones.

Mervyn Davies again led by example, and we all followed him and listened to his every word. The Pontypool Front Row dominated their opponents, and the lock forward pairing of Allan Martin and Geoff Wheel were superb, and getting better with every game. Behind them, Terry Cobner and Trefor Evans formed a formidable back row with Mervyn Davies. What a squad of players we had, with an abundance of talent in all positions. The signs looked good for a big year in 1976 in the Five Nations Championship.

9

Wales 1976-77

'With JPR, JJ, Gareth, Gerald and myself, we a great backline that was full of talent and the confidence to play running rugby from any area of the pitch. Steve slotted right in, knowing we had the ability to turn defence into attack, as was summed up by 'that' try against Scotland at Murrayfield in 1977. We were under pressure in our half when the ball was stolen in a maul and instead of kicking to touch, JPR received the ball, fed it to Steve who passed to Gerald, then Dai Burcher, then Steve again, back to me and we scored under the posts. Not only did it take the Scots confidence away, but it was voted the best try ever scored in Five / Six Nations history! Steve had a good temperament on the pitch which made his goal kicking skills look fairly relaxed and stress free. Ray Gravell was quite the opposite, full of nervous energy, but together they were a great partnership in midfield which complimented the talents they had either side of them. We had a great team spirit throughout this period, both on and off the field and had a fantastic time, playing winning rugby and enjoying some serious socialising together off the field.'

Phil Bennett (Wales, British & Irish Lions)

While many millions enjoyed watching the Wales team win numerous Triple Crowns and Grand Slams on the television, and hundreds of thousands went to the games at the Arms Park, Twickenham, Murrayfield, Lansdowne Road and *Parc des Princes*, hundreds –

sometimes thousands – also turned up to watch our weekly training sessions held every Sunday on Aberavon Beach.

The competition for places in the starting XV was so fierce, those sessions were exhilarating yet brutal affairs and the fans who came to Aberavon were treated to some real tough battles, as players strived to impress the selectors and secure their place for the next game. Over and above the head-to-head fights for selection supremacy, though, the team spirit was amazing and the players all acknowledged our squad ethos that if, for any reason, a player had to withdraw from the team, his replacement was expected to slot right in, like a cog in a finely tuned machine.

The first game in the 1976 Championship was against England at Twickenham and a controversial team selection created red-hot debate in Wales. Phil Bennett had been dropped, with the selectors opting for John Bevan and David Richards, a 20-year-old playing for Swansea, acting as cover. As it turned out, however, both picked up injuries between the squad announcement and the game, meaning that Phil was drafted back in at outside-half.

The English side had recently dispatched Australia 23-6, so looked a team that was going to be very tough to beat, but JPR had another view. That game at Twickenham would see him become the most capped full-back in Welsh rugby history, with 34, passing the 75-year-old record of Billy Bancroft, and he'd clearly decided that, if needs be, he was going to take on England on his own and break the record in style. JPR was outstanding – a one-man army who blitzed the men in white. He was so strong and determined, it felt that if the other 14 of us had gone off at half-time he would have held England at bay, on his own, for the whole of the second half. JPR scored two tries – he loved scoring tries against England more than any other team – and Gareth Edwards scored one, to equal the Wales try-scoring record. I managed to kick three conversions, with Allan Martin scoring a long-range special penalty kick. It was a great day for JPR and Wales with a resounding 21-9 victory.

During this period I had the dubious pleasure of rooming with Allan Martin, the Aberavon second rower. We ended up as roommates for around five years, and what an eventful five years they were. I'm just happy to have lived to tell the tale.

The WRU protocol for all home internationals was for each set of two roommates to stay at the Angel Hotel in the centre of Cardiff, opposite the Arms Park. On match-day, however, your wife and friends could use the room and your roommate would get another room for their wife and friends. The fact that this was the standard procedure saved me a few years later, when the WRU received a letter from a woman who was trying to get hold of me. She wanted to thank me for such a great night in Cardiff after an international. It turned out an amorous fan had impersonated me to impress the young lady during a night 'on the town', but the fact I was definitely in the Angel Hotel with my teammates saved me a potential divorce!

Imagine my surprise, one Sunday morning after a game against England, when the hotel manager accosted me on the steps outside the Angel. He insisted that I accompany him to the room as it was was a total wreck, and there was also a substantial bill for beer and wine consumed during and after the game, all charged to the room! I protested my innocence, and after asking around, I found out that Allan had moved out of our shared room, booked another room, but had given them the keys to our room! I refused to pay the bill and was given a severe talking to by the WRU. You always had to keep an eye on that Allan Martin. Otherwise, you easily could be out of pocket for the whole weekend on international games. He earned his nickname 'Panther' because he was always looking for an opportunity to help himself to what he fancied.

Our coach, John Dawes, was not a disciplinarian. He trusted his players to look after themselves and expected us not to let him or the team down. On the Friday night before a home game we were expected to go to a cinema in Cardiff city centre, with the WRU covering the cost of a choc-ice, before returning to the Angel Hotel to relax for the rest of the evening. John was a firm believer that the team, once back at the hotel, should do what they normally did on a Friday night before playing for their clubs. That being the case, those of us who usually had a few beers before a game were encouraged to do the same. We were sensible, though. If we were playing France the following day, and knew we'd be chasing their three-quarters around the pitch the next afternoon, then the last thing you wanted was a belly full of beer to carry around with you. John trusted you to do the right thing because if you ever let him or yourself down, then there were several players itching to take your place and give it their all if you were not prepared to.

During my years playing international rugby it was interesting to see how my illustrious teammates prepared for games, physically and mentally. Whether their focus was their diet or a specific routine, it varied greatly from player to player. John Bevan would eat a whole beef steak at lunchtime, only an hour or so before kick-off. He'd usually throw it up on the field in the middle of the game, mind, but he never altered his routine. I couldn't eat a thing on a match day and would just drink a few cups of tea. Phil Bennett used to have a glass of sherry and a few eggs – yes, I know! It looked revolting, but his performances for Llanelli, Wales, and the British and Irish Lions were always of the highest quality.

After our resounding victory at Twickenham, the next game was was Scotland in Cardiff. We were all unhappy about our defeat the previous year, and I certainly wanted some revenge for my enforced night in the Edinburgh Royal Infirmary! Scotland had recently beaten Australia, England and Ireland, and had a wealth of talent in their backline, such as Andy Irvine, Billy Steele, Jim Renwick, Ian McGeechan and Dougie Morgan. Up front, they had some exceptional players including Ian McLaughlan, Sandy Carmichael and Gordon Brown, so they took the field as a formidable opposition, but there was only ever going to be one winner on that day.

There is always a unique atmosphere for the Wales v Scotland game in Cardiff. Scottish supporters travel down in their thousands and have long-standing twinning arrangements with rugby clubs through the valleys and towns of Wales. The atmosphere is heightened with the sound of bagpipes and the sight of the kilts as both sets of supporters mingle and exchange their Celtic banter in the pubs, clubs, hotel bars and restaurants of the Welsh capital.

A comfortable 28-6 home victory was the payback we'd been looking for, with Gareth Edwards, Trefor Evans and JJ Williams each scoring a try. Phil Bennett scored 13 points, with three penalties and two conversions. The atmosphere was unbelievable in the stadium. The supporters loved every minute and spilled out of the ground to celebrate in the city centre.

Having beaten England and Scotland, we headed to Dublin to play Ireland and hopefully secure the Triple Crown. There was one change to the team, with Tom David replacing Terry Cobner. It turned out to be a dominant display of open rugby on a day when Phil Bennett had an inspirational performance at outside-half, scoring 19 points on his own. In a breath-taking display of 15-man rugby, when our physically exhausting training sessions on Aberavon Beach paid dividends, our preparations and tactics were perfect and all came together in a perfect performance on the pitch at Lansdowne Road.

Gareth Edwards continued his sensational run by scoring another try. Phil also scored a try, and Gerald Davies scored two more, both very stylish, as only he could. It was a joy to line up inside Gerald as part of the Wales back line of the 1970s. We just needed to pass him the ball in a bit of space and then admire his mazy running as he worked his way down the field. Gerald's side-step was legendary, but even if opponents knew it was coming he'd be too quick for them. It was great to witness the style and talent of the man. Ireland had the likes of Tom Grace, Mike Gibson, Moss Keane and Willie Duggan but it wasn't enough and we enjoyed an emphatic 34-9 victory.

The Triple Crown now secured, all thoughts turned to the final game of the Championship, against France in Cardiff, and the potential Grand Slam. France had a very talented side and were inspiringly led by Jacques Fouroux, their diminutive scrum-half. France had a skilful and powerful pack and were the pre-tournament favourites to challenge Wales as Five Nation winners. With Cholley, Paco, Paparemborde, Imbernon, Palmie, Rives, Bastiat and Skrela, the French pack was some unit. Some years later, Fran Cotton told me it was the best pack of forwards he had ever played against. High praise indeed.

The game was a battle of attrition. Trying to contain those French forwards was very difficult, and when they succeeded to get the ball to their talented backs we knew we'd be up against it. The Welsh forwards, led by Mervyn Davies, had to be at their best to compete with them, and it was a real baptism of fire for Cardiff's prop forward, Mike Knill, who made his debut as a replacement.

What a match it was. France went 7-0 ahead when I was tackled in midfield and tried to throw a pass to Gerald Davies while lying on the ground. It was a poor decision, as I mistakenly threw the ball to Jean-Pierre Romeu, who moved it onto Jean-Francois Gourdon who scored in the corner. I knew I'd made a terrible error and was determined not be remembered as the player who ruined Wales' Grand Slam challenge.

We knew what we needed to do and the home crowd roared us on. Every single player upped their game and we took the French on in every department. It was beautiful, yet brutal, rugby.

JJ Williams scored a try and Phil Bennett and I each kicked two penalties, with Allan Martin kicking a long range effort. We had come from behind to be leading 19-13 as the match entered its closing stages. It could still have gone either way. JPR then produced a defining moment when he saved a certain try by shoulder-charging the French winger, Gourdon, into touch, just inches from the try-line. In what would have been a certain red card and penalty try in modern rugby, JPR's clenched fist celebration told the French all they needed to know – there would be no way through the determined Welsh defence. A few minutes later the referee's whistle was drowned out by the deafening roar of the delirious Arms Park crowd. We had won. The Grand Slam and the Championship were ours.

Welsh rugby's exhilaration turned to devastation just 22 days after that famous Grand Slam victory when our inspirational captain Mervyn Davies suffered a brain haemorrhage while playing for Swansea against Pontypool in a Welsh Cup semi-final and was forced into an early retirement. 'Merv the Swerve' was a special man, a great captain and a prodigious rugby player. His boots would be huge ones to fill.

There were several changes to the team as we started the 1977 Five Nations Championship campaign. Newport's Dai Burcher made his debut in place of Ray Gravell, while Neath prop, Glyn Shaw, replaced Charlie Faulkner. The back row was changed entirely, with Ebbw Vale's Clive Burgess and Newport's Jeff Squire coming in for their debuts, while Derek Quinnell was given the unenviable task of replacing Mervyn Davies. The captaincy was handed to Phil Bennett.

The first game was against Ireland in Cardiff, and it was a close game until the superiority of the Welsh forwards began to tell in the last quarter. With some decent ball from the forwards, the backs paved the way for two excellent tries from Gerald Davies and JPR, while Clive Burgess scored a try on his debut. The victory was marred somewhat, though, by the sending off of Geoff Wheel and Willie Duggan for fighting. There was a rumour that the pair spent the second-half in the nearby Old Arcade pub having a beer together. From knowing those two, it would not surprise me at all! Phil Bennett scored 10 points, and

70

I managed to kick a drop-goal after receiving a questionable dive-pass from Bobby Windsor. A 25-9 win was a great start to the defence of our title.

Next up was France, which had the usual big-game atmosphere at *Parc des Princes*. The French were just too good on the day, and their powerful pack gave us a right going over for 80 minutes. We were second best in both skill and forward power and the final score of 16-9 didn't reflect the French team's superiority. Their captain, Jacques Fouroux had a field day and the French back row of Rives, Bastiat and Skrela harassed the Welsh backs all over the pitch, including Newport's winger, Gareth Evans, who made his debut as a replacement in very tricky circumstances. France kept us in a stranglehold and fully deserved their victory. Skrela and winger, Dominique Harize, scored the two tries for France, and all we could respond with was my three penalties.

During the game I recall Phil Bennett getting trapped at the bottom of a ruck. Bastiat must have thought he'd won the lottery and succeeded in getting in a few nasty digs. He was a real menace all afternoon, but pushed it too far later in the game when he purposefully trampled on Clive Burgess' head at a breakdown. I saw the incident and in my rage, and wanting to gain some retribution, sneaked up on him from the side and smacked him in the face. Now, in the films, when someone gets punched hard in the face their legs crumple and they keel over. Bastiat just turned to me and snarled – he didn't even flinch! I hastily made my retreat thinking, 'Sorry Clive, he's all yours!' Bastiat, however, wasn't going to let my intervention go unanswered and caught me a few times before the end of the game. He extracted his revenge on me with a few well chosen punches, as his teammates added points to the scoreboard. We were well beaten in both senses of the word.

Battered and bruised we limped back to Cardiff to prepare for our next game, against England at the Arms Park, and we were much the better side that day. The only change to the team was Aberavon's prop forward, Clive Williams, who made his debut replacing Glyn Shaw. We ended up scoring two tries through JPR, who would have loved to have played against England every week, and the other by, who else, Gareth Edwards. I kicked two penalties to England's three, and the win put us back on track for another Triple Crown.

The England game is remembered for Phil Bennett's pre-match 'Look what those bastards have done to Wales' speech, when he went on a tirade of how Wales had been colonised and stripped of its coal, water, steel and homes by England for centuries, ending with the infamous line, 'What have they given us? Absolutely nothing. We've been exploited, raped, controlled and punished by the English – and that's who you are playing this afternoon'. Those kinds of statements can work on some, but it did not stir me up anymore than I was already. I did not need such things. Grav was in tears (no surprises), and voicing his agreement with Phil, and a few others were getting fired up. Geoff Wheel just sat there whistling or singing as he always did, Geoff is a great guy. I remember after Phil delivered the speech, the Chairman of Selectors Keith Rowlands said that if we could get that vital win today and beat England, we could then "march with confidence" onto our next game in Scotland. Geoff turned around and said marching to Edinburgh would be knackering so couldn't we just fly up like other people, which caused much laughter among the players, completely ruining Keith's motivational pep-talk. Geoff did not buy into those things: give him the shirt, point him to the field, and that was all he ever needed.

As usual, it was a fabulous game of open rugby on an exceptional Murrayfield surface. The Scottish side put us under a lot of pressure just as one would expect from the home team, but one particular move changed the course of the game and more or less settled the result. In 2020 it was also voted the best-ever try in the history of the Five / Six Nations Championships.

We were under pressure in our own half when JPR managed to get hold of the ball but offloaded to me after being robustly tackled by Sandy Carmichael. I sensed the space outside of me and threw a pass to Gerald Davies, which was never a bad idea! Gerald put in a fantastic side-step, followed by a huge hand-off of Douglas Morgan before passing onto Phil Bennett. Phil took it up to almost halfway before moving the ball onto Dai Burcher who had raced up in support on the right wing. Dai, with two Scottish defenders racing back to him and with him heading towards the touchline, looked inside for support. By this time I had tracked the move and was now inside Dai, who delivered a clever overhead pass to me. With the Scottish lock forward charging towards me I quickly off-loaded to Phil who only had Sandy Carmichael the Scottish prop in front of him. It wasn't a fair contest as a step from Phil saw him speed away to score under the posts. Well, that try just about finished the Scots. They had been attacking, dangerously, deep in our half and within 10 seconds they were under their posts watching Phil convert his try.

That try was voted Wales' best try ever, and was made even more memorable by the brilliant commentary from the legendary broadcaster, Bill McLaren. It just showed what intent and belief that the team had in attack. Whenever we had a chance to play, someone in the three-quarter line would produce a 'rabbit out of the hat', with a moment of brilliance. It was no fluke or coincidence that Phil Bennett was also involved in the famous Barbarians try against New Zealand in 1973, which saw him starting a move deep in his own half that was ended gloriously by Gareth Edwards or, as the late great Cliff Morgan refers to him in his iconic commentary, "That fellow, Edwards".

The final score at Murrayfield that day was 18-9 which meant we had won the Triple Crown for the second year running. JJ Williams also scored a try in the game and Phil ended up with 14 points.

After the game we had a dinner function and sat next to me was Bernard Wright, my former lecturer at Borough Road College. Bernard was now lecturing in Scotland, and it was great to see him after all these years. During our conversation he said to me, "You're not trying to tell me you meant that pass are you? It was a fluke, wasn't it?" Slightly taken aback I said, "You're having a laugh, aren't you? Of course I meant it." Bernard would have none of it, though. Having seen me play at Borough Road he couldn't believe I'd developed the skills to deliver a pass like that. Thanks, Bernard!

In three short years with Wales, I had won a Grand Slam and two Triple Crowns. It was a fantastic start to my international career and I was incredibly fortunate to be surrounded by so many great players. I could not rest on my laurels, though, and had to maintain my form or my place in the Wales team would be gone.

10

Wales 1978

'The sight of this stockily built anticipator of colleagues' needs and opponents' errors was a familiar one from the mid-1970s. Where the play broke down or a subtle touch was required, there Fenwick's shock of blond hair would be. Neither of these men won praise for the brilliance of their running but their contribution to the years of unparallelled triumphs to come was undeniable for they exemplified the solidarity of Welsh teams clinically able to contain, weaken and then surge away in a final flourish. Gravell's hot-blooded charges to the post were complemented by the equally ferocious, yet sanguine, Fenwick who gave the impression of having iced spinach in his veins. No one had had international nerves so cool and steady since Barry John whose Welsh points record first Bennett, then Steve Fenwick, took to giddier heights.'
Dai Smith and Gareth Williams (*Fields of Praise, The Official History of the Welsh Rugby Union*)

The 1978 Five Nations Championship began with a game against England at Twickenham. The selectors brought Ray Gravell back into the centre to play alongside me. Charlie Faulkner also returned to the side, meaning that the Pontypool Front Row was reunited. Jeff Squire joined Terry Cobner and Derek Quinnell in a powerful back row. Not only did we have a formidable team, but we were also brimming with confidence.

The pitch at Twickenham was a bog that day, nothing like Murrayfield with its underground heating which provided an excellent playing surface irrelevant of any inclement weather. The game was not a showpiece, but the forwards slogged it out in the mud and we fought hard for a 9-6 win, which was decided by penalties. Alastair Hignell, the English full-back kicked two, but our captain Phil Bennett kicked three penalties to gain us the victory.

Having Grav back alongside me was great, and what an ardent Welshman he was. Before games, he would get so nervous and be in such a state that many of us just could not understand. Before one game, he was sat looking at a card and burst into tears. Charlie Faulkner walked up to Grav and asked him what the matter was. "It's a card from Toodles, my cat," replied Grav, "to wish me luck." Charlie turned away, shaking his head in disbelief, and walked over to Bobby Windsor. "He's got a fucking card, off his cat!" Grav was emotional playing club games for Llanelli, but when he was playing for Wales it went stratospheric!

Scotland at the Arms Park was the next challenge, and we put in a convincing display, running out 22-14 winners in yet another entertaining game with the Scots. Gareth Edwards scored his 20th, and final, try in a Welsh jersey. I also scored a try, as did Ray Gravell and Derek Quinnell. We now faced two tough games to win a third consecutive Triple Crown, a feat that had never been previously achieved.

We knew Ireland in Dublin was going to be a tough slog. Wales seldom won at Lansdowne Road, but little did we realise how hard and brutal it was going to be. The Irish team was fired up, and it turned out to be one of the most physical battles I have ever been involved in. Ireland tore into us right from the kick-off, with Phil Orr, Moss Keane, Willie Duggan, Stewart McKinney and Fergus Slattery leading the way. Tony Ward and Mike Gibson were quality backs with no intention of finishing second best. The rucks and mauls were not for the faint-hearted. It was simply a case of who could jump the highest and stamp the hardest! It was a real struggle but we managed to win the game 20-16. I had a good day with a try, and four penalty goals, and JJ Williams scored the decisive try. It was a great feeling to make history and win the triple Triple Crown.

Despite the elation of knowing we'd achieved something very special, the changing room was quiet and the atmosphere was very muted. The sheer exhaustion and the bumps, cuts and bruises being attended to by the physios meant that a celebration was furthest from our minds at the time.

Many members of the team had given everything for Wales for well over a decade and the fatigue of highly competitive international rugby had finally taken its toll. It was no surprise that Phil Bennett and Gareth Edwards decided to finish their international careers in that Dublin changing room. They were truly world-class rugby players who added new dimensions to the global game, as well as being incredible servants to Wales.

So, yet again, the final game of the Championship was a shoot-out between the two most successful teams in the recent history of the Five Nations. The magnificent French stood between us and winning the Grand Slam at our beloved Arms Park in front of our army of supporters who couldn't conceive defeat as an option on Welsh soil.

International day in Cardiff is an experience that all lovers of rugby truly savour. The tens of thousands of fans who make their way to the Welsh capital always create an inspirational atmosphere. The encouragement, the loud vocal support and, above all, the singing made us feel unbeatable.

With a packed National Stadium roaring us on, we ran out onto the field knowing the harsh reality that we needed to achieve something we'd failed to do the previous year in Paris – to match the beauty and brutality of French rugby. They had a fantastically talented backline to compliment their uncompromising forwards, including that brilliant back-row trio of Jean-Pierre Rives, Jean-Pierre Bastiat and Jean-Claude Skrela. There was one change to the Welsh team that had played in Dublin, with Gareth Evans coming in for JJ Williams.

Skrela scored an early try, but our forwards responded by getting stuck into the French pack and took control of the game. The mercurial Phil Bennett was fantastic. He scored two tries and one conversion. The other international 'retiree', Gareth Edwards, scored a drop goal, as did I with one that wobbled around and squirmed just over the bar. For Gareth and Phil it was a grand finale to their international careers. Gareth produced one of his best performances of his long international career, with his sublime tactical kicking and ultra-reliable service to Phil, whose performance was inspirational, and whose ten points guided us to a memorable 16-7 victory. We had won the Grand Slam again, for the third time during the 1970s and twice in three years. It was Wales' eighth 'Slam' which was a tournament record.

After the on-field celebrations with our euphoric fans we all trooped off the Arms Park pitch and slumped to our seats in the changing room – utterly exhausted. For a few minutes there was total silence as we caught our breath and nursed our wounds. Then the beer began to appear and the mood lightened as we relaxed and acknowledged our achievement. The respect we had for the French players was immense and it was something they reciprocated fully. That year we played Australia on tour and New Zealand at home, when we were the better team, but the hardest match we played that year was undoubtedly *Les Bleus* at home. Their brute force and unbelievable flair was an irresistible combination and they were by far our most difficult opponents. The All Blacks had the ability but were well structured and hardly ever played instinctive off-the-cuff rugby, so were very predictable. The only thing predictable about the French was their unpredictably, with their forwards handling the ball as confidently as their backs. We also enjoyed each other's company and with Jean Pierre Rives leading the way, thanks to his excellent English, we had a great night in Cardiff.

Within weeks of that unforgettable day in Cardiff we were off on tour to Australia with Terry Holmes and Gareth Davies replacing Gareth Edwards and Phil Bennett, two world-class rugby half-backs, possibly the best ever as a partnership in world rugby. The Cardiff pair would have surely felt the intense pressure to slot into the team and perform against Australia but they did a great job, as did Terry Cobner who took over the captaincy from Phil.

Beating Australia is a tough ask at the best of times, but the questionable decisions made by the Australian referees without a doubt influenced games and particularly contributed to Wales losing the second Test. The fact that Australia had already won the first Test with some questionable refereeing made it a very frustrating tour.

When we played Queensland in Brisbane just before the first Test, referee Bob Burnett, who was also on the Queensland committee, showed his true colours and the writing was on the wall. Don't get me wrong, Queensland were a good side and half of the team playing that day had recently beaten a touring All Black side, but they were not unbeatable for the Five Nations Grand Slam champions, with three consecutive Triple Crowns.

Early in the game, after a scrum had been awarded, our scrum-half Brynmor Williams who'd not heard the call clearly, checked with the referee, "Whose ball is it"? Showing his annoyance that his call had not registered with the Welsh player, Burnett impatiently shouted back "It's ours!" This alleged slip of the tongue left us in no doubt where his loyalty lay. Later, he tried to send off Geoff Wheel for an alleged head-butt. Geoff did no such thing but did have a nervous tick which saw him jerk his head from time to time. The referee was out of his depth, unable to cope with the pressure and should never have been allowed to officiate his own side's game. We were furious and threatened to walk off if he sent Geoff off. There were so many other incidents during that game when Burnett was not refereeing fairly, so we must have played well to secure the 31-24 win.

The two Tests were both keenly contested matches, Australia's team were definitely on the way to becoming a top side with the likes of Laurie Monaghan, Andrew Slack, Paul McLean, Greg Cornelsen, Mark Loane and Tony Shaw in their ranks. In the first Test, we had the Cardiff pair, outside-half Gareth Davies and flanker Stuart Lane, making their debuts, alongside and Newport scrum-half Brynmor Williams. We out-scored the Aussies two tries to one, thanks to Gerald Davies and Brynmor Williams, but we gave their outside-half, Paul McLean, lots of kicking opportunities by conceding too many penalties. He took took full advantage and we ended up losing 18-8. Some of the referee's decisions were harsh but the Australians deserved the victory.

The second Test was, however, an absolute farce due to the blatant biased refereeing. It wasn't simply a case of us being penalised unfairly, as their players were getting away with violent foul play with the referee turning a 'blind eye' to their conduct. Steve Finnane, the Australian prop forward who had his hands taped like a boxer, smashed Graham Price from behind with a vicious right hook which shattered his jaw. It was nothing less than common assault that would have led to a criminal conviction in a court of law, which is ironic considering that Finnane was a barrister! Pricey had to be replaced by Aberavon's John Richardson, who won his first cap.

Losing players of Graham's calibre made our task much harder considering that we were already struggling with injuries before the game. Alun Donovan, the Swansea centre, was forced to play his debut at full-back and, when he also got injured after only a few minutes of the game, his replacement Gareth Evans sustained a broken cheekbone making his first tackle in the game. Despite suffering an injury that would have normally seen him leave the field of play, JJ Williams had no option but to hobble around with an ankle injury just to ensure we had enough bodies on the field; it was a crazy situation!

WALES 1978

We were in such dire straits that the starting back row for the second Test consisted of Stuart Lane at flanker, Newbridge's Clive Davis – a lock forward making his international debut – was selected at eight, and JPR – arguably the world's finest full-back – played flanker, which made him very proud. There cannot be many who have played as a back and a forward in international rugby, but then JPR was not your typical rugby player. Scrum-half, Terry Holmes from Cardiff, also made his debut.

Despite all these injuries, we still outscored Australia by two tries to one, thanks to our captain, Gerald Davies, and Terry Holmes, but the penalty count went against us again. We were robbed right at the end by a Laurie Monaghan drop goal which looked, to most of us, to have gone at least four yards wide of the post. That was good enough for the referee who immediately signalled a score. We lost 19-17 and the hard-earned win we believed we'd deserved, in what turned out to be Gerald Davies' last game for Wales, became a disappointing defeat. Captaining the side for the only time on his final appearance for Wales, and scoring a try, wasn't quite enough for the perfect send-off for one of rugby's great players.

Australia was a lovely country to visit, particularly Sydney and Brisbane which were fantastic cities, with New South Wales and Western Australia also stand-out places. While we were in Perth we had the pleasure of a trip on Sir Edward Heath's yacht, *Morning Cloud*, during a yacht race in which we finished in 32nd place, much to the disgust of the crew who fancied their chances of winning. It was another loss we suffered in Australia!

The vast size of Australia was astonishing – it took four hours to fly from Perth to Sydney – but it was our game against Northern Territories that showed us the huge contrast in climate and geographical expanse of the country. The venue for the match was the only rugby pitch with its own dam, which fed water onto the pitch to maintain it: a beautiful green patch in the middle of an arid expanse of desert-like land. The game, however, had almost been cancelled the previous day because of the worst storm to have hit the area in over 40 years. Then, the day after the game, two Aussie farmers arrived at our hotel and were surprised to see us checking out. They asked what was going on so we told them that we were leaving because the game had been played the day before. They were devastated and told us they had driven 700 miles just to watch the game, but were a day late! A 1,400 mile round trip for nothing!

The Australian people were friendly but there still seemed to be an undercurrent of resentment towards the 'Pommies' as they called us. The Aussie rugby supporters were more than slightly biased in their opinions and certainly not shy in making them loudly known. Ray Gravell, the most exceptional example of a true Welshman, got a taste of this when we played Sydney at the city's famous SCG cricket stadium. Our match was the third of three games played that afternoon so the crowd were well-oiled with beer, and as we we ran down the concrete ramp onto the pitch a supporter who was hanging over the wire fence with a can of beer in hand yelled "Go home, you Pommie bastard" at Ray. His studs screeching as he came to an immediate halt, Ray faced the spectator and asked, "What did you call me?" Standing his ground, the fan replied "A Pommie bastard", to which Ray said, "You can call me a bastard anytime, but never call me a Pommie bastard. I'm Welsh and proud of it!" The stunned Aussie supporter apologised profusely and looked a little puzzled as we went off to complete our warm-up!

In November 1978, we had the opportunity to play New Zealand, who were touring Britain and Ireland. Any fixture with the All Blacks was the ultimate test in rugby union, and after a strong Five Nations Championship, we relished the challenge. JPR Williams was named as the captain and Llanelli's flanker, Paul Ringer came into the side for his debut, teaming up with Jeff Squire and Derek Quinnell in the back row. Ringer's searing pace in the loose brought us a nice mix in the back row and was a real asset.

With two well-matched sides, the game was a very close-run contest and it went right down to the wire. Late in the second half Wales were leading 12-10, from three penalties from Gareth Davies and one from myself, and we probably deserved the win. Still, the All Blacks found a way to win, and it came in the form of a lineout ruse delivered by Andy Haden and Frank Oliver. As Bobby Windsor threw the ball into the lineout, Haden and Oliver both 'fell' out of the line as if they'd been pushed by Welsh players. The truth was they had conspired to dive out of the line to deceive the referee, Roger Quittenton, into giving New Zealand a match-winning penalty opportunity. The plan worked perfectly. Haden theatrically dived out of the line as if he'd been hit by a sniper, quickly followed by Frank Oliver. Quittenton blew for a foul, claiming that Geoff Wheel was leaning on Oliver, but as my teammate, and roommate, Allan Martin later commented, Geoff and Frank had been at it all game without any intervention from the referee. I firmly believe that Frank, who we all now know had discussed a last-minute act of skulduggery with Haden, indulged in football tactics by over-exaggerating the contact with Geoff which triggered the referee into giving a penalty. He conned the referee plain and simple. It could be said that the incident illustrated the clash of old-school amateurism in the form of Roger Quittenton, who was too naive to ever imagine a rugby player making such a blatant attempt to mislead him, and the win-at-all-costs 'professionalism' of the All Blacks. It was a disgrace. Brian McKechnie scored the penalty to give the All Blacks a narrow 13-12 victory. It was an incredibly frustrating ending to a fabulous game of rugby.

Don't get me wrong, New Zealand rarely field a poor side and that team of 1978 was a class outfit, but we believed that we were the better team and deserved the victory. We were champions of the northern hemisphere having won the Grand Slam a few months earlier. The changing room was silent for quite a while as we gathered our thoughts. We felt as if we'd been kicked in the guts, denied our first win against the All Blacks since 1953 and, worst of all, there was nothing we could do about it. It was just so brazen. The fact that the players later wrote about the incident in a book and openly admitted their plan to dive out of the line is still hard to stomach, but we just had to take it on the chin. We assumed there'd be another opportunity to avenge the defeat before too long, but it turned out to be the closest Wales would get to beating the All Blacks until 2004 when we again lost by a single point (25-26). For me, that was the best chance I'd ever had to beat New Zealand wearing a Wales jersey.

At the after-match dinner that evening, the Welsh players were still very annoyed at being cheated out of a famous win as we sat down opposite the New Zealand players. There was definitely a bad atmosphere as we dined face-to-face with our opponents, until Geoff Wheel cut through the tension when he loudly requested in front of all the players, "Andy, could you dive over here with the salt, and you Frank, can you dive over here with the pepper!" It melted the ice-cool atmosphere and brought laughter from both sets of players. Losing to New Zealand in that manner is still a huge regret in my rugby career, even after all these years, we were so close, yet they found a way to win.

11

Wales 1979-81

'Playing at outside-half with a 'no tackle' philosophy meant that I required centres I could trust 100%. Steve Fenwick was unquestionably such a centre. Steve had all the skills and was reassuring to play alongside because in addition to doing his job expertly, he would look out for his teammates. He was one of the most unselfish players I ever played with, who possessed a golden match-winning talent for creating a last-minute try or taking long-range goal-kicks which inevitably split the posts. Steve Fenwick is a top man.'
Gareth Davies (Wales, British & Irish Lions)

With Phil Bennett and Gareth Edwards retiring after the Grand Slam victory, and Gerald Davies calling time on his international career in Australia, the 1979 Five Nations Championship squad contained several new faces from the team that had beaten France in Cardiff the previous year. Elgan Rees from Neath replaced Gerald Davies on the wing, while the Cardiff half-backs, Terry Holmes and Gareth Davies, kept their places following the tour to Australia and home defeat to the All Blacks. Once again, JPR Williams was selected as captain.

The campaign started against Scotland at Murrayfield where a try each from Terry Holmes and debutant Elgan Rees, and 11 points from three penalties and a conversation from myself, secured a good 19-13 win by, over a spirited Scottish side.

A home game against Ireland was next up, when we ran out 24-21 winners thanks to tries from Allan Martin – his only try for Wales – and Paul Ringer, and I scored 16 points with four penalty goals and two conversions. It was a close game and a real thriller, which we managed to sneak over the finishing line.

The game against France in Paris was another dog-fight with *Les Bleus* squeezing out a narrow 14-13 victory. Swansea duo, Barry Clegg – replacing Geoff Wheel at lock – and David Richards – in place of Ray Gravell in the centre – both made their debuts. The Pontypool Front Row played their 19th game together – a Welsh record. What a trio. Terry Holmes scored a try, and I scored nine points with three penalties, but it was not enough to gain the win and the dream of two consecutive Grand Slams was over.

The 'Decade of the Dragons' ended with a convincing win over England at the Arms Park. Alan Phillips, the Cardiff hooker, and Clive Griffiths, Llanelli's full-back who came on as a replacement, both made their debuts. Composure at half-back, complete dominance upfront and a committed defence enabled Wales to beat England 27-3, our biggest win over England since 1905. Elgan Rees, David Richards, Paul Ringer and Mike Roberts all scored tries, as did, of course, JPR Williams – we were playing England after all. It brought us the Championship, our 21st, as well as our fourth Triple Crown in four years. As individual records go, JPR and I had played in all of the Triple Crowns games and in every game of the 1979 Five Nations campaign. I also equalled the Championship points record with 38, which I shared at the time with Phil Bennett, England's Roger Hosen, and Ireland's Tony Ward. It was a remarkable decade for Welsh rugby, and I am so proud to have been a part of it.

The following season witnessed a new coach and a new captain for a new decade. John Lloyd, a former Wales player and a Bridgend man through and through took over as coach, while Jeff Squire was appointed captain. Several players from the 'Golden Era' had been, and continued to be, replaced, leaving me Graham Price, Allan Martin, Geoff Wheel and Jeff Squire as the remaining experienced internationals. Among the new players coming into the set-up were Swansea full-back, Roger Blyth who replaced JPR Williams (talk about a difficult task), Llanelli centre, Peter Morgan, Aberavon winger, Les Keen, and Pontypool number eight, Eddie Butler. All bar Roger

Blyth, who had been capped in 1974, made their debuts in the 1980 campaign. The Welsh side was almost unrecognisable to what it had been two years previously.

The first game of the campaign, against France at the Arms Park, ended in a 18-9 win, with tries from Terry Holmes, Graham Price, Elgan Rees and David Richards. This win set another record. It was the 23rd consecutive Five Nations home match without defeat, beating the previous record, set by Wales during the first golden era in the first decade of the century.

We then travelled to Twickenham to play England, in an infamous match remembered for being a very dirty game of rugby. The press had hyped-up the game all week and political tensions were high as the spending cuts announced by Margaret Thatcher's new Conservative Government were hitting Wales – that hadn't voted Tory since 1865 – particularly hard. Both teams were desperate to get the victory for rugby reasons but there was a lot more going on in the background. With the intense build-up and increased scrutiny on the game the referee was under a great deal of pressure, and it took only around 15 minutes for our flanker Paul Ringer to be sent off for foul play. It was a debateable decision which resulted in us playing with 14 men for over an hour.

I saw the incident quite clearly and remember it well. As the England outside-half John Horton was kicking the ball clear following a lineout on halfway, Paul ran towards him intending to block the kick but caught him awkwardly late with an outstretched arm – some would say it was an elbow – knocking John Horton backwards, holding his head. The Irish referee, David Burnett, had only recently warned the two captains, Bill Beaumont and Jeff Squire, to control their respective players following a spate of niggly and ugly incidents when punches had been thrown and heads stamped on. Blood had flowed and the referee had finally run out of patience.

Despite the sending off, the first at a Five Nations game at Twickenham for over 50 years, unsightly incidents were happening at regular intervals as players squared up to defend themselves and their teammates. At one stage, Terry Holmes and John Scott had to be pulled apart during a serious confrontation, and they were both teammates with Cardiff at the time! There was foul play from both sides and it wasn't a good advert for rugby union.

England ended up winning 9-8, with three penalty goals from Dusty Hare outscoring our two tries from Elgan Rees and Jeff Squire. After the dust settled, Paul Ringer was banned from playing rugby union for eight weeks and only played one further game for Wales. It sadly defined the international career of a very talented player, whose misdemeanour was pretty minor compared to many others that occurred during the afternoon. It wasn't a game to be proud of in so many ways, but my lasting memory was John Horton, who had been a former flatmate of Paul Ringer, coming over at the end of the game to apologise to Paul for the sending off incident.

After the disappointment on that dark day at Twickenham, Wales welcomed Scotland to Cardiff and it was good to be back playing open rugby. We got a good result, winning 17-6 with tries from Terry Holmes, Les Keen and David Richards.

The final game of a poor season saw us losing 21-7 to Ireland in Dublin. We were very mediocre, while the Irish were convincing victors. Roger Blyth scored a try but we fully deserved to lose with that type of showing. In my opinion, it was the worst performance of my previous five years playing for Wales. We showed no fight against the ever-spirited Irish. Our opponents had caught us up and worked out how to beat us. They had bridged the gap we'd created a decade earlier and the loss of so many of our quality players – true legends of the game – was obvious to all. The success of the 1970s was truly gone and the the prospects for the 1980s didn't look good.

With the Five Nations thankfully behind us, I was incredibly honoured the following September to be named as captain for a non-Test Welsh XV against an invitational Overseas XV in Cardiff which formed part of the WRU's centenary celebrations. Even though it was a non-capped international, leading your country out at the National Stadium was a special feeling. In an open and entertaining game, we beat the invitational side – containing Romanian, Canadian, Japanese, Argentinian, American and Fijian players – 32-25, with full-back Roger Blyth helping himself to 24 points, including three tries. A very impressive individual tally.

Two months later we again played the New Zealand All Blacks, and I retained my role as team captain. It was a great distinction to captain my country in a full international, and against the All Blacks. I felt very proud indeed. The game against New Zealand was nothing

85

like the 1978 match, when we deserved to win. On this occasion we were no match for a far superior New Zealand team and suffered a heavy 23-3 defeat. It was the biggest defeat of my Welsh international career, which was bad enough, but taking such a thumping in my first game as Wales captain, was not the great start I was hoping for! Gareth Williams, my teammate at Bridgend, made his debut at number eight, in this match as did London Welsh winger, Robert Ackerman. Playing against the All Blacks is always memorable and, for Gareth and Rob, even though we were soundly defeated it was still a moment to cherish.

Later that month, to continue the WRU's centenary celebrations, a Wales & England XV faced an Ireland & Scotland XV, and I was selected to captain the Wales & England team. With the Queen and Prince Phillip attending as honorary guests of the WRU, my role meant that I was to greet Queen Elizabeth and introduce her to the players. I was told that when addressing the Queen I was to call her Ma'am, but apart from that I wasn't given any other real instructions. That was a recipe for disaster.

I stood on the pitch at the head of my team, all lined up wearing the specially produced red and white quartered shirt, waiting nervously for the Queen to walk out to meet us. At the appointed time she appeared and, initially, all went well as we shook hands and greeted each other. "You must be very proud to be captain of this Wales and England team," the Queen said. "Extremely, Ma'am," I replied. "We don't normally mix with the English, but we will give it a go. We will make an exception for today." My attempt at gentle rugby humour didn't have quite the response I was expecting. If looks could kill I'd have been spending the night in the Tower of London before being taken to the gallows. The Queen looked at me in livid astonishment, walked off and never spoke to me again that day! Nantgarw banter and royalty don't mix.

It was a Barbarians-type game with plenty of tries and both teams throwing the ball around, attacking at every opportunity from everywhere on the field. Even though it was an exhibition match, we still wanted to win. Let's face it, England hadn't won in Cardiff for decades so the English players had a huge incentive to perform, while for the Welsh players, defeat at the Arms Park was unacceptable. For me, I was captain and didn't want to lose two consecutive games, so I was so pleased to have won the game 37-33. I hoped our victory had secured my captaincy of the Wales team but, after my chat with the Queen, any hopes for a knighthood had disappeared as fast as the Queen did before the game. There would be no Sir Steve Fenwick!

My hopes of retaining the captaincy were realised, and to be appointed as captain of Wales for the 1981 Five Nations Championships, during the WRU's centenary year, was a huge privilege. It was an incredible honour and a source of immense pride, for me and for my family.

I had been very fortunate to have played under several exceptional captains, and I was determined to lead and inspire in the same way they had inspired me. Mervyn Davies led by example, but he then expected his players to take responsibility for themselves – he inspired us but the onus was on you. Benny didn't say much but when he did, like that infamous speech before the England game, we all listened. It was an absolute pleasure to play under his captaincy, for Wales and the Lions. Terry Cobner was tactically very astute and knew the 10-man game he played at Pontypool wouldn't suit the expansive game we played for Wales. We needed quick ball and he demanded a fast service from the forwards. I knew that some players responded to a rousing pre-match team-talk and some didn't, but all players respected a captain who led by example and that was the type of captain I tried to be.

The first Five Nations match was against England at the Arms Park, and after the previous year's 'Battle of Twickenham', it thankfully settled down to a hard but sportsmanlike game of rugby. A few new faces were playing for Wales with Llanelli winger, David Nicholas, my old friend, Bridgend prop forward Ian Stephens, and Cardiff flanker, Rhodri Lewis, all making their debuts. In addition to the newcomers, we had an old face back in the ranks in the unmistakable shape of JPR Williams who came out of international retirement to reclaim the number 15 jersey. In a very close and highly competitive game, which we won 21-19, lock forward Clive Davis scored our solitary try. I managed to kick a conversion and four penalties, with Gareth Davies adding a drop goal. I had my first victory as captain of Wales in a full international, and against, of all people, the old enemy, England! It is fair to say that I was pretty happy.

Next up for us was Scotland at Murrayfield with Maesteg's full-back Gwyn Evans making his debut as a replacement. It was Scotland's day, dominating in all facets of play, and they deserved their 15-6 victory. Although I was disappointed, I was pleased for my old friend Jim Renwick, the renowned Scottish centre, as it was the last time I would face him in the international arena. Jim was such a laid-back character. He treated games like he was just out on a Sunday stroll. We had some great battles over the years, but he still found the time to talk to me during breaks in play. In the previous year's Five Nations game in Cardiff, while the forwards were going down for a scrum, he shouted over, "Hey, Steve! Where are we going later, is it the same place as last time." I like to be in my own bubble during a match so shouted back, "Piss off Jim. I'm trying to concentrate here." There was no offence meant, he remains a good friend.

With the loss against Scotland, we could not now win the Championship, and the selectors agreed that the time was right for some new players to be brought into the team, to see if they were ready for international rugby. I went from the high of beating England, as captain, to being discarded after the following game! It did hurt to be dropped, especially as team captain, and I also found the decision not to make any changes in the forwards surprising, as Scotland had beaten us up front, but you have to accept these decisions. It turned out to be my last rugby union international for Wales as indeed it was for JPR Williams, one of the all-time rugby greats who, throughout his international career for Wales, never lost against England. What a player and what a record.

The baton had now been passed to a group of younger players as the selectors sought to build a new side. The Llanelli centre Peter Morgan was brought in to replace me, while the Bridgend pair of outside-half Gary Pearce and scrum-half Gerald Williams also won their first caps. Maesteg's Gwyn Evans returned at full-back. They were later joined by the Cardiff centre, Pat Daniels, and the Swansea duo, flanker Mark Davies and lock forward Richard Moriarty.

The captaincy was handed to Jeff Squire and my short-lived, three-match tenure as captain ended with one win and two losses. It's not the highest win ratio, but being captain of my country is something I will always cherish and be very proud of.

The final two games for Wales ended with a narrow 9-8 victory at home against Ireland, where Gwyn Evans and Gary Pearce both got on the score sheet with Gwyn scoring two penalties and Gary dropping a goal to kick Wales to victory. With Gerald Williams also winning his first cap that season, having both Bridgend half-backs in the national team was quite an achievement for my club side.

The final game was away in Paris where Wales lost 19-15 to a good French side, with David Richards scoring a try and Gwyn Evans kicking a conversion, and three penalties. It was, overall and personally, a pretty disappointing Five Nations campaign for Wales, particularly during its centenary year, but the side was going through a rebuilding phase after many years of outstanding success.

My Welsh rugby union journey was over. I had played for six fantastic years, winning 30 caps and scoring 152 points for my country. I feel very privileged and honoured to have represented my country, and for it to coincide with such a golden period for the national team is something I'll be forever grateful for.

12

Lions 1977

'Although the 1977 Lions tour to New Zealand wasn't the most successful tour that I have been part of, the life-long friendships formed within the touring party remains one of my finer memories. In addition to Steve's gutsy and resolute performances in midfield was his wonderful sense of humour, regardless of the difficult circumstances we faced. The great Welsh teams of the 1970s made life extremely difficult for all their opponents but playing against good guys like Steve made another defeat almost bearable!'
Peter Squires (England, British & Irish Lions)

After getting established in the Wales side in 1975 and 1976, the next target I set for myself was to be selected for the British and Irish Lions tour to New Zealand in 1977. It was, and still is, the pinnacle of rugby union if you played for one of those four nations. I was well aware of the exploits of the previous tours of the 1970s, when exceptional Lions teams won the 1971 series in New Zealand and the 1974 series in South Africa. The Lions had created rugby history on both tours and I wanted the opportunity to achieve the same. I had become a Dragon and now I was determined to become a Lion.

From 1970 to 1977 Wales had been a real force in the Five Nations, winning two Grand Slams, three Triple Crowns, and winning the Championship on five occasions (two of them shared with other nations) so I really thought I had a good chance to be selected for

Lions v New Zealand, 1ˢᵗ Test, 1977. Kicking for touch as Bill Osborne attempts the charge down.

Like all tours, the Lions played hard and made the most of the plentiful hospitality.

Left: Hawkes Bay v Lions, 1977. Terry Cobner in possession.

Below: Gordon Brown, leading the singing.

The 2nd Test. Having a friendly disagreement with Laurie Knight.

The lull before the storm - a pre-Test match pitch walkabout with Brynmor Williams, John Bevan, Clive Williams, David Burcher and JJ Williams.

With David Burcher & Bill Beaumont.

In good cheer on the plane, with David Burcher, Peter Wheeler and Trefor Evans.

Post-match relaxation with Gordon Brown, Moss Keane, John Bevan, David Burcher and Tony Neary.

S. P. FENWICK
Bridgend RFC. Centre-threequarter. 5ft 10in. 13st 2lbs. Won first cap against France in Paris in 1974/75 season. Now holds 12 caps. Long range goalkicker. Married schoolmaster. Hobbies reading and art. Age 26.

Left: Some of the players took a few liberties with those writing the programme notes. For those who know me, reading and art have never been top of my list of interests!

Right: Lions v Fiji - Gareth Evans, Jeff Squire and me posing for a photo with the Fijian police. The weather was wonderful, and so much better than the mud bath conditions in New Zealand.

THE
1977
LIONS

Andy Irvine   Bruce Hay   Peter Squires   Gareth Evans   John Williams

Elgan Rees   Mike Gibson   Ian McGeechan   David Burcher   Steve Fenwick   John Bevan

Bryn Williams   Douglas Morgan   Derek Quinell   Willie Duggan   Trevor Evans   Jeff Squire

Tony Neary   Terry Cobner   Bill Beaumont   Allan Martin   Gordon Brown   Maurice Keene

Fran Cotton   Graham Price   Clive Williams   Phil Orr   Peter Wheeler   Bobby Windsor

The initial Lions squad of 30 players created controversy for including 16 Welshmen. By the time of the 4th Test, the depleted squad of 29 featured in the match programme still had 15 Wales players.

We lost the 4th Test, and the series, at Eden Park, but we should have won and drawn the series 2-2. The teams were equally matched and a drawn series would have been the fair result.

Lion #512 - my original Lions jersey was destroyed in the fire that destroyed the Taff's Well RFC clubhouse, so I was extremely grateful when the Lions sent caps to all the players. It takes pride of place at my home in Groeswen.

After our return from New Zealand we played a one-off game at Twickenham as part of the the Queen's Silver Jubilee celebrations. Playing against JPR was a novel experience.

A few years later, and another royal occasion. Gren's wry Welsh rugby humour says it all: 'We should have known better than to get a chap from Bridgend to design it.'

In 1979 I went into business with my good friend Tom David. Thankfully, it was very successful and we eventually sold the company. We enjoyed working together and made it a real family

affair as can be seen in this photo of a company celebration with my parents, Wendy, Brenda and Jim.

Kate, aged one, with her proud parents at a fancy dress event in Groeswen. Kate won a prize for her elf costume.

Christmas Day, with Kate and Siôn.

Enjoying a family holiday in France.

Margaret, my lovely Mum.

Kate and Wendy, 1978.

All boys together - relaxing with (R-L) my brother Mark, his son Jack, and Siôn.

The Fenwick family in the late 1970s: (L-R) Chris (my elder brother) and Marsha; Dad and Mum; Ann (my sister) and Ken; Wendy and me; Caroline and Mark (my younger brother).

The business was doing well and I had won many awards for my rugby, but I wanted a new sporting challenge, so with the support of my wonderful wife I decided to follow my ambition and switch codes to rugby league.

The confidential discussions with David Watkins about switching codes, held in a pub in Ogmore-on-Sea, remained confidential for less than 10 minutes! What Tom David and me were doing was so obvious. Unlike most Welsh code breakers, I went 'north' by going south, to Cardiff Blue Dragons.

Above: Dai Watkins assembled a number of former Union players including Tom David, Paul Ringer and Brynmor Williams, and we all looked forward to seeing how we'd adapt to League.

Below: It was tough! I signed as a professional on 27 August 1981 and played my first game, against Salford at Ninian Park, three days later. It was a very steep learning curve.

After a few months in RL with the Blue Dragons, I was lighter, stronger and fitter than I'd ever been before. It was a real eye-opener to the professionalism of the 13-a-side game. The long bus journeys to and from the north of England for our Sunday matches helped us to bond as a team and created an unbreakable camaraderie between the players, and the management.

For me, with business interests in south Wales and a young family happily settled in Groeswen, I couldn't have moved to a northern English club, so the formation of the Blue Dragons suited me, and others, perfectly. I loved it.

Above: Union and League may be two different games, but scoring a try is exactly the same, as is place-kicking, so I settled down to my new role quite quickly.

Below: Scoring a try against Dewsbury at Ninian Park. After the early high crowds the attendances at games fell dramatically, as the lack of spectators on the terraces shows.

Another bonus of switching codes was that I, once again, played for Wales. The first of my two games for Wales RL was against England on 8 November 1981 at Ninian Park, when I kicked four goals in a 20-15 defeat. Playing alongside me that day were (top left, L-R): Mel James, Glyn Shaw, Tom David, Gordon Pritchard, Adrian Cambriani, Danny Wilson [Ryan Giggs' father], Ness Flowers, Martin Herdman.

Enjoying a round of golf with my son Siôn at Wenvoe Golf Club.

Kate and Siôn live fairly close, with their partners Craig & Danielle, so we often meet up for family celebrations, such as my 70th birthday in 2021: (L-R) Danielle, Craig, Kate and Wendy.

It was a proud moment when, in 2019, I was inaugurated into the Welsh Sports Hall of Fame 'Roll of Honour' by my two former teammates, Graham Price and the much missed JJ Williams.

Looking across the valley, from Groeswen to Caerphilly. From here I can see where I was born, where I went to school, where I worked as a teacher and where I first played rugby. I've always loved living here. It's home.

the 1977 Lions Tour. Dai Burcher and I had been a successful centre pairing for the 1977 Five Nations Wales side that, under the captaincy of Phil Bennett, had won their second consecutive Triple Crown after winning the Grand Slam the previous year. We had beaten all the other 'Lions nations' over the previous two years and many observers expected a large contingent of us to be selected for New Zealand.

When the 30-strong British and Irish Lions squad was announced, 16 Welsh players were selected, with Phil Bennett named as captain. Dai Burcher and I were delighted to be chosen in the centres, alongside Ireland's Mike Gibson and Scotland's Ian McGeechan. Five players each from England and Scotland and three from Ireland made up the remainder of the squad. With 53% of the squad being Welsh, the announcement certainly raised eyebrows. The media in Ireland, Scotland and England had plenty to say, with the English media in particular protesting that having 16 Welshmen wasn't justified and contravened the Lions' ethos of having a more balanced representation from the four unions. In my opinion, however, if the Lions are serious about winning a Test series, the selectors must opt for the best players on offer, irrespective of nationality. Wales was by far the most successful side during that period, and the selectors' decision was fully justified.

The 16 Welshmen initially selected were Phil Bennett, John Bevan, Dai Burcher, Gareth Evans, myself, Elgan Rees, Brynmor Williams, JJ Williams, Terry Cobner, Trefor Evans, Allan Martin, Geoff Wheel, Graham Price, Derek Quinnell, Clive Williams and Bobby Windsor. JPR Williams, Gareth Edwards and Gerald Davies all announced that they were unavailable for the tour due to family or work commitments otherwise there could have been even more Welshmen selected. How the English media would have loved that!

Before departure, however, Geoff Wheel had to withdraw on medical advice and was replaced by Ireland's Moss Keane, and Jeff Squire replaced England's Roger Uttley who aggravated a back injury at a Lions training session before we departed. During the tour itself Pontypool's Charlie Faulkner and Alun Lewis from London Welsh flew out to join the touring party which further boosted the Welsh contingent. A very fine scrum-half, Alun never went on to play for Wales and, alongside Brynmor Williams and Elgan Rees, was one of three uncapped Welsh players.

I'd be asked to confirm my availability to tour but that didn't mean my selection was a done deal, so when the news broke of my selection the atmosphere at the school was electric and an impromptu party was organised at my local pub, the White Cross in Groeswen. It was a fantastic way to celebrate that I was heading to New Zealand. It was an incredible honour.

The whole squad, including coaches and back-room staff, totalled 42 which, when you take into account we flew out on 10 May and returned on the 19 August after playing a four-Test series against New Zealand and a single Test match against Fiji, it is not a big group at all. The Lions tours of recent years have much larger set-ups. Our back-up staff included a manager, Scotland's George Burrell, and John Dawes, the Welsh national coach who, in 1971, had captained the Lions to its first – and only – series win in New Zealand. Believe it or not, we had to borrow a physio for the tour, Doc Murdoch, who was a great guy, and New Zealand allocated us a baggage man!

Back in those days rugby union was an amateur sport, with all the players having full-time jobs, so taking almost four months off work was a big commitment and had a financial impact on many players. It also put a strain on the companies and organisations we all worked for, with many not overly happy at losing key members of staff for a third of a year. I was fortunate that, as a teacher, the school allowed me the time off and the local education authority – Mid Glamorgan – agreed to maintain my full salary whilst I was on tour. Other teachers from other authorities were not so lucky, as Jeff Squire found out when Gwent refused to match Mid Glamorgan's generosity and he had to accept financial hardship in order to fulfil his rugby ambitions. The road to New Zealand wasn't paved in gold as our 50p daily allowance, enough for a coffee and a sandwich (I know that is hard to believe) testifies. In terms of kit, we were given two jerseys but had to bring our own boots for the tour. Looking back on it now, those aspects of the tour epitomised the realities of amateurism but, for us, it was a dream come true and we all did it for the love and honour of playing for the Lions.

The squad contained 11 players who had been on the previous Lions tour, to South Africa, but only three remained from the victorious 1971 trip: Derek Quinnell, Gordon Brown and Mike Gibson, who was on his fifth Lions tour, an amazing achievement. We felt we had a good robust set of forwards who would be a match for New Zealand, and our backs – including Andy Irvine, Peter Squires, Ian McGeechan, Bruce Hay, JJ Williams, Phil Bennett – with good clean ball in the right positions, could be the key to unlocking their defences. What we did not take into account, no one could, was that New Zealand was going to have one of the wettest winters in their history, which produced some atrocious conditions to play rugby. The plan of having talented backs who could give the All Blacks the run around by playing open, flowing rugby stopped in its tracks due to the weather.

New Zealand is a wonderful country to visit, especially if it's rugby related. The people there just couldn't do enough for us. Whether on North Island or South Island, the welcome was second to none. It was the best country I have ever toured in my life, and we had over three months in a dream world, playing the game we loved against the best team in the world. It was a special time in my life, and we were amateurs, financially, but we were treated like professionals wherever we went. The players from England, Ireland, Scotland and Wales bonded brilliantly, and we tried our utmost to achieve a series win.

We had some real characters in the squad and none more so than the Irish pair of Willie Duggan and Moss Keane. The two loved a drink and hated training. Who could blame them in the horrible, wet conditions we encountered? They quickly hit upon a master plan to avoid training sessions. Getting into the hotel lift together, on their way to training, the two huge Irishmen would jump up and down to damage the lift's mechanism and bring it to a halt with them trapped inside. By the time an engineer came out, the lift was repaired and they appeared in the hotel lobby, the duo had missed a good hour and a half of training. Genius!

This happened a few times, and John Dawes knew something was going on. Finally, the lift got stuck yet again with Moss and Willie trapped between floors. A few of us were in the foyer of the hotel, just about to head off to training, and heard a hotel employee shout up to the pair, "Don't worry, an engineer is on his way." We then heard a muffled but very clear Irish voice as Willie shouted back down, "Stuff the engineer, get some beer and sandwiches in here!" We were all in hysterics.

After losing the Test series in 1971, which had a massive impact on the pride of the rugby-obsessed nation, the New Zealand media was full of stories and commentary that 1977 was the time for revenge. We knew what was being said in the media, but without them hyping-up the series, we were well aware that we had a real battle on our hands to achieve what we came for – a series win, pure and simple.

From the first game to the last match of the tour, it was hard going. The quality of New Zealand rugby from the provincial contests to the Tests was of a very high standard, and the itinerary was brutal. Facing Canterbury, Otago and the New Zealand Maoris was tough going, but they were just the mid-week games! On Saturdays we faced the likes of Hawkes Bay, Wellington, and the All Blacks themselves, as the 25-game tour pushed us to the very limit of our endurance. It was a thorough examination of our rugby ability and prowess. It was to our credit that the 1977 Lions improved throughout the tour, and were the equal of their much-vaunted opposition.

We played nine games before the first Test, losing only once, against New Zealand Universities, in the mid-week match before the first Test. Along the way we had played some good rugby and scored some excellent tries, with Andy Irvine scoring five against King Country. The forwards, led by Terry Cobner who also acted as the forwards' coach in training, were impressive and dominated many games. We felt in good shape going into that first Test, even if a lot of training sessions were on waterlogged fields that resembled marshes in the crazy conditions we faced on that tour.

Every player wanted to be named in the Test team and I was no exception, but I assumed that the Gibson and McGeechan centre partnership were likely to be selected so there'd be no place for me. Two brilliant players with huge experience, they were the favourites, I thought. With nine gruelling games before the first Test, we just got on with the matches, one-by-one and none of us ever really got a hunch if we would play in the Tests. The only real indication you had was if you played mid-week then it was unlikely you'd play at the weekend.

When the time came for the announcement of the team for the first Test at Wellington there was no great fanfare – George Burrell just read out the squad in a team meeting. Imagine my surprise and delight when I heard my name being called out. I was over the moon. The side selected for the first test against New Zealand was: 15, Andy Irvine; 14, Peter Squires; 13, Ian McGeechan; 12, Steve Fenwick; 11, JJ Williams; 10, Phil Bennett; 9, Brynmor Williams; 1, Phil Orr; 2, Bobby Windsor;

3, Graham Price; 4, Allan Martin; 5, Moss Keane; 6, Terry Cobner; 8, Willie Duggan; 7, Trefor Evans.

The build-up to the game took a strange twist when the actor Warren Mitchell appeared in the changing room for a chat with the players. Filming in New Zealand for a television programme, he'd driven to the ground in a Rolls-Royce before blagging his way in to see the players before the game. Mitchell, who famously played the fouled-mouthed West Ham fan in the popular yet controversial television series *Till Death Do Us Part*, clearly loved his rugby and wanted to wish us all the best for the Test series. He was great with us, and his unexpected visit was a welcome few minutes' break from the intensity of the pre-match preparations.

'Windy Wellington' lived up to its nickname, and the conditions were atrocious as a bitterly cold wind blew in from the sea. We got off to a great start when Andy Irvine kicked a huge, morale-boosting, long-range penalty from within our own half. As the match approached half-time, New Zealand had scored two tries, one from scrum-half, Sid Going and the other from prop forward Brad Johnstone, but with Phil Bennett responding with three further penalties, we were 12-10 ahead.

Just before the interval, from a maul within our half, Brynmor Williams made a great break through the All Blacks' defence and passed inside to me. To my right we outnumbered the All Blacks' defence and I sensed that a try was on, so I passed the ball onto Trefor Evans who was immediately tackled and threw an underarm flick pass out to Phil Bennett. A split second later, Grant Batty, the New Zealand winger, intercepted the pass and sprinted 60 yards to score, evading Graham Price and then Andy Irvine, who valiantly chased him into the in-goal area. The try was converted and when the referee blew for half-time, we went in 16-12 down. I am not putting any blame on Trefor. There was a chance to go wide and potentially score a try. It is one of those things, but key moments cost us throughout the tour. The second half was scoreless. We had lost the first Test.

After defeat in the opening game of a four-match Test series, we simply had to win the second Test if we were to win the series outright. It was a must-win match requiring a do-or-die effort from every player. The changes to the team reflected the heightened importance of the game with, in the backline, JJ Williams switching wings and Gareth Evans given an opportunity on the opposite wing. A new-look pack saw five changes, with Fran Cotton replacing Phil Orr, and Peter Wheeler handed the hooking duties from Bobby Windsor. Allan Martin and Moss Keane were replaced by Bill Beaumont and Gordon Brown, and Derek Quinnell came in for Trefor Evans.

The game was played at a muddy Lancaster Park, Christchurch. The Lions showed the necessary commitment to beat New Zealand and get the tour back on the road. We got the edge in the forward battle and all credit to the pack for that. JJ Williams scored a good try when he stepped inside the New Zealand defence that had over-committed while coming across to try to stop him. After we got the lead we defended resolutely, and won 13-9, with Phil Bennett scoring another three penalties. It was now one win apiece and the sought-after series win was back on. I'll never forget a comment from Terry Cobner as we left the field. A man of few words, despite being a teacher, Terry hardly ever gave me a compliment but on that day he turned to me and said, "Little man, big heart." That meant a lot.

Before the third Test, we gained victories against New Zealand Maoris, Waikato, New Zealand Juniors and Auckland, so we built some real momentum going into the game, and we were growing in confidence that we could take the lead in the series. With the forwards winning the up-front battle in Canterbury all eight kept their positions and there was just the one change to the backs, with Dai Burcher coming in for Ian McGeechan.

The third Test was played at Carisbrook, Dunedin, where the pitch had so much surface water on it that, on the morning of the game, a helicopter was called in to hover over the pitch and disperse the water. Being Welsh I thought I knew all about rain but I'd never seen anything like it, day-in and day-out, in New Zealand. On the day, the All Blacks were the better side and deserved their win. We had chances, missing several kicks at goal, but lost 19-7 with New Zealand scoring two tries through forwards, Andy Haden and Ian Kirkpatrick, with Willie Duggan scoring a consolation try for us and Andy Irvine kicking the one penalty.

It was a hugely disappointing day. New Zealand was now 2-1 ahead with one game left. The aim to win the series outright had now disappeared, but we still could come away with a drawn series. The starting XV saw further changes with, in the backline, Elgan Rees coming in for JJ Williams, Ian McGeechan reclaiming his place at the expense of of Dai Burcher, and Dougie Morgan replacing Brynmor Williams. The only changes to the pack were in the back row, where Jeff Squire and Tony Neary replaced Terry Cobner and Derek Quinnell respectively.

We were relishing the opportunity to draw the series, and were the better side. Dougie Morgan scored a try with a close-range burst, which he also converted, and kicked a penalty. As the match headed into injury time we were 9-6 ahead when a cruel piece of luck went New Zealand's way. Bill Osborne put in a harmless looking kick which caused some confusion in our defence when the ball bounced unpredictably, before the All Blacks won back possession. Our hooker, Peter Wheeler, then ripped the ball out but it fell straight into the hands of New Zealand's number eight, Lawrie Knight, who gratefully gathered the ball and dived over the try line. New Zealand had won the match 10-9, right at the death.

We could easily have drawn the series but, with that last-ditch Lawrie Knight try, we had lost the series, 3-1. It was devastating. We were the better side in two of the tests, but just did not take our chances and also had some moments of misfortune that went against us. From a personal perspective, I had played in all of the Tests and played in 17 tour games. Even though we had lost the Test series, playing for the Lions is something I am very proud of. It was such a privilege and a fantastic experience.

Two days later a demoralised Lions squad arrived in Fiji, a country baking under a scorching hot sun. We had finally found dry, warm weather! We all headed to the pool and commandeered the sun loungers, and the bar staff. Drinks began to flow as battered bodies sought recuperation and pasty complexions soaked up the Pacific sun. Legend has it that a number of the Lions, and some British journalists, racked up a $700 bar bill while enjoying ourselves with a few drinks. I cannot confirm or deny this.

The unofficial Test match was played in Suva the day after the 'few drinks around the pool' episode. The side selected was: 15, Andy Irvine; 14, Gareth Evans; 13, Ian McGeechan; 12, Dai Burcher; 11, Phil Bennett; 10, John Bevan; 9, Alun Lewis; 1, Charlie Faulkner; 2, Bobby Windsor; 3, Graham Price; 4, Bill Beaumont; 5, Allan Martin; 6, Tony Neary; 8, Jeff Squire; 7, Trefor Evans. I was not included in the starting XV – I cannot say I was too disappointed – but I was named on the bench. Fiji were a decent side, especially on their rock-hard ground, and we lost the game 25-21, with tries for the Lions scored by Phil Bennett (playing on the wing), Bill Beaumont and Dai Burcher. It was slightly disappointing to end the tour like this, but as Fran Cotton summed up afterwards, "Next time can we arrange a 12-week tour of Fiji with a one-week stopover in New Zealand?"

Only just over three weeks after we returned home, the 1977 British and Irish Lions were reunited for one final game. As part of the Queen's Silver Jubilee celebrations, and a charity fund-raiser, a contest was organised pitting the Lions against a Barbarians side consisting England, Ireland, Scotland and Wales players that were not in the original Lions touring party, plus players from France. It was a pretty strong line-up!: 15, JPR Williams; 14, Gerald Davies; 13, Ray Gravell; 12, Charles Kent; 11, Dave McKay; 10, David Richards; 9, Gareth Edwards; 1, Barry Nelmes; 2, Duncan Madsen; 3, Mike Knill; 4, Bob Wilkinson; 5, Geoff Wheel; 6, Jean-Pierre Rives; 8, Jean-Pierre Bastiat; 7, Jean-Claude Skrela.

The British and Irish Lions side was: 15, Andy Irvine; 14, Peter Squires; 13, Steve Fenwick; 12, Ian McGeechan; 11, Gareth Evans; 10, Phil Bennett; 9, Dougie Morgan; 1, Fran Cotton; 2, Peter Wheeler; 3, Graham Price; 4, Bill Beaumont; 5, Gordon Brown; 6, Tony Neary; 8, Willie Duggan; 7, Derek Quinnell.

It was a great game to play in with some fantastic tries. I managed to score a try as did Gareth Evans and Andy Irvine. The Barbarians responded with great tries from JPR, Ray Gravell and Dave McKay. It was sparkling rugby played on a beautiful sunny day at Twickenham. The final score was a 23-14 victory to the British and Irish Lions. Over £100,000 was raised for charity as well, making it a great occasion all-round, playing with and against some great friends.

When people look back at the 1977 series in New Zealand there have been many things said and written about how we should have won the series, and questions asked over such things as too many Welshman selected, queries over the coaching, the captaincy and other matters. In my opinion, who knows what would have happened if we'd had JPR, Gerald Davies and Gareth Edwards available to play. In those tight encounters would the moments of magic players like that can conjure up have made the difference? Quite simply, we don't know, but even without those stars, we could have tied the series, and possibly won, with a bit of luck being on our side, also some dry weather with suitable hard surfaces might have helped as well!

Several writers and some players on tour such as Peter Wheeler, who played in three of the four tests, have all stated that the Lions forwards outplayed their counterparts in all departments and that the Lions backs weren't good enough to take advantage of this. My response to this as one of those backs is to say it is true. We possibly could have done marginally better behind, then the result could have been different, but what the forwards who state this, including my mate Peter Wheeler, fail to see is that in the four Tests the All Blacks' forwards scored four tries to the Lions forwards' solitary try. So, if the Lions forwards were so dominant, where were the tries? It's funny how backs and forwards seem to look at things differently in this fabulous game of rugby union. Ultimately, we had lost the test series, and that was a massive disappointment to all of us involved.

In 1980 I got another opportunity to play for the Lions, this time in South Africa, and I was approached to check my availability before the squad was announced. I had just gone into business with Tom David and felt it would be unfair to go off on a rugby tour for over two months when we were trying to get the company up and running. Also, my daughter Kate was only a few months old and I knew Wendy would have appreciated my support around the home, so I declined the invitation.

After I had turned down the invite, I was asked to meet up with the man who was to coach the Lions that year, Noel Murphy. Noel came to Old Deer Park, where I met him after I had played for Bridgend against London Welsh. He was very kind and was keen for me to tour and even suggested that I came out to South Africa for just the four Test matches. It was a generous gesture but, again, I declined due to my family and business demands, plus I felt going out for only the Tests was unfair on the rest of the playing squad and would not have been good for team morale. As it turned out, the Lions lost the test series 3-1 to South Africa, and I don't think my inclusion would have made any difference!

13

Touring the World

'I had the pleasure of getting to know Steve when we were both selected to play for the Barbarians on their tour of Canada in 1975 and were roommates for three weeks. Who would have thought that a guy from Taff's Well, would win a then-record 30 international caps at centre, play for the Lions in all four Tests against New Zealand in 1977, score 38 points in the 1979 Five Nations to equal the Championship record, and lead the Wales team as captain in 1980. Steve is a very witty and engaging person with a wicked sense of humour and a person I have a great deal of admiration for.'
Gareth Jenkins (Wales 'B')

One of the great perks of playing rugby union is being able to tour with invitational teams such as the Barbarians and Crawshays. I have had the honour of participating in these tours and enjoyed them very much because they provided wonderful opportunities to meet players from other teams and countries. They also helped open my eyes when meeting players I'd not got on with while competing against them in internationals and club games, such as Peter Squires, Peter Wheeler and the much-missed Bruce Hay. As soon as we met up on tour we just clicked and remained good friends. Those tours enabled so many former opponents to become great friends as we bonded through socialising as well as training and playing. Tours were essential for both rugby values and personal enjoyment.

TOURING THE WORLD

I first played for the Barbarians in Redruth, Cornwall. It was a hot September afternoon when I drove to Cornwall for an evening fixture and when I got to the hotel where the Barbarians were staying I was knackered, and I thought I would have a nice cold pint of lager to quench my thirst. I didn't pay much notice to two men dressed in dark red jackets and caps who turned out to be senior Barbarians committee members. As I ordered my pint of lager, one of the men walked up to the bar and said to me, "Oh no, you don't!" Thinking he was reprimanding me for drinking lager before the game, I gave him a mouthful and told him where to go! He patiently waited for my rant to end, looked straight at the barman and told him to give me my money back and that all further drinks would be 'on the house'. I just burst out laughing and apologised. What a great set-up the Barbarians is. You are there to enjoy yourself on and off the pitch. It's outstanding, and I hope it never changes.

I was also selected for the Barbarians' Easter tour of Wales in 1976 and then, just a month later, to travel to America and Canada. Both were fantastic tours with great people. The Easter tour used to typically entail playing Penarth on Good Friday, Cardiff on Saturday and then Swansea on the Bank Holiday Monday. Fans used to turn up in their thousands to be entertained with attacking rugby, and they were rarely disappointed. It was great to meet up with your mates and catch up with what was happening in English, Irish and Scottish rugby. Penarth frequently played the role of lambs to the slaughter on Good Fridays. Fortunately for Penarth, the BaaBaa's socialising on the Thursday night before the game often got a bit excessive, giving them more than a slight chance of a surprise victory.

The night before the Penarth game, we all went socialising and drinking in Cardiff. Mike Knill, the Cardiff prop forward and Welsh international, who was also selected to be playing the following day for the Barbarians, took us out on the town. Mike knew every publican and club owner in Cardiff due to his work as a police officer in the area and, after many different venues and many drinks late at night, we ended up playing snooker and having yet more drinks. It was now well past midnight and Mike was playing snooker against Brynmor Williams, who is a great mate of mine, yet both were due to be playing later that same day against Penarth! Halfway through a snooker frame, Brynmor stopped playing, excused himself and left the table.

He was gone quite a while, and when we went to see where he was, we found him being violently sick in the toilet!

After our big night out in Cardiff, it was no surprise to me to see what unfolded the following day in Penarth. The Penarth team and their supporters couldn't believe what was happening on the field and I felt so fortunate to be watching from the stand! While Mike, Brynmor and others were doing their best to perform, I knew how ill they must have been feeling. It was to be a huge upset, with Penarth winning the game on merit. I vividly remember Mike being physically sick on his own 25-yard line, while the game was going on at the other end of the pitch! I also recall Brynmor as he was just about to score a potentially match-winning try after making a break from his half. He had broken through the Penarth defence, with nobody near him, before he lost possession of the ball and it bounced into the stunned spectators standing on the touchline. Whether a lack of concentration, or the ten pints of lager sunk the previous night, fair play to Penarth who rejoiced in their victory against a star-studded Barbarians team. The rest of the Easter festivities went well, but that game against Penarth will always stick in my mind.

Another unforgettable moment was during the tour to North America in May and June 1976, when we played in the Boston Bi-Centennial Tournament. Duncan Madsen, the Scottish hooker, was captain for the first game and was trying to build us up to fever pitch in the changing rooms so we would be bursting to get out onto the field and show them how good we were. The problem was that we didn't need it! We were all experienced players who knew their jobs on the pitch, and we were confident we would get the win. He was ranting and raving like a man possessed and at the very end of his tirade, he grabbed his right boot and kicked it as hard as he could to show us he meant business. Unfortunately, the aggressive team talk backfired badly when his right foot connected with the changing room door, went right through it and left his foot totally stuck – him on one side of the door and his foot on the other. The players collapsed in laughter. It was so funny and, to increase his embarrassment, he had to wait for someone to come and free his foot from the door, which meant we kicked off and had scored 12 points before he appeared on the touchline ready to continue inspiring us with his captaincy.

TOURING THE WORLD

The Barbarians committee were on top form in North America and were rarely seen without an aperitif in their hands. They enjoyed the tour as much as, if not more than, the players. After one training session, Geoff Wheel was struggling again. The issue Geoff had was that he had been called up for the tour at the last minute, as an injury replacement, but his off-season had comprised of him being a frequent visitor to the Swansea Dockers Club for a few beers! Geoff Windsor-Lewis, the honorary secretary of the Barbarians and former Wales international centre, took charge of training, and it was hilarious, as he would line us all up for a series of 100-metre sprints against the likes of Andy Irvine and Dave Shedden, so Geoff Wheel was finding it challenging to say the least.

Now beginning to lose his cool, Geoff reacted badly when Windsor-Lewis called a rerun on one of the sprints because Geoff's feet had been over the starting line. Geoff was just trying to get a start on the other, far faster, players and avoid the embarrassment of being last again. It wouldn't have made any difference to the result of the sprint but the coach was adamant, saying, "Geoffrey, your feet were over the line! So, as a punishment, when we finish today, can you please collect all the corner flags on the field." No surprise, Geoff was quick to respond to this request, "Ok, coach, jump on my back, and I will give you a fucking piggyback all around the pitch." That level of sarcasm left Geoff Windsor-Lewis miffed at the end of a tough training session in 90-degree heat.

After training, we had some decent leisure time so Brynmor Williams, me and Geoff Wheel decided to have a look around Boston. Upon arrival in Boston we had been advised not to go to Boston Docks, known locally as the Combat Zone for obvious reasons. After that description it was the main place we wanted to visit so we booked a taxi and headed straight for it! As we approached the docks and got out of the cab we could see how rough the area was – a man was lying on the street with blood spurting out of his head. It looked like he had been shot! Brynmor and I immediately turned to get back into the taxi, but Geoff had beaten us to it and was already in the back seat pleading with the taxi driver to get us out of there and back to the hotel. For the rest of the time we were in Boston, Geoff never came out of his hotel room unless for training and matches. The only question he asked whenever we knocked on his door was, "Is it rough where we are going?"

Before one of the games we played in Boston, against a team called BATS, Bay Area Touring Side, Geoff Windsor-Lewis decided to give several opposition players a lift to the stadium on our team bus! Something none of us had ever seen before. Part of mentally preparing for a game was to build-up the image of the 'enemy' you were about to play against, but here we were giving them a lift! Geoff stood at the front of the bus and said: "We are giving some chaps from the BATS a lift to the game today, and please give them a jolly good welcome." Geoff Wheel was well into his pre-match build-up and wasn't at all impressed: "BATS! I'll give them BATS, I'll BAT their fucking heads in!" The journey passed off without any incident and we came out on top as comfortable winners.

The tour proceeded to Canada, and after one sweltering morning training session in Calgary, the decision was made that the players were free to do what they wanted for the rest of the day. Knowing that the players gave everything during the games and in training, the Barbarians encouraged players to enjoy the whole experience of touring, which provided wonderful memories for the rest of your life. Geoff Wheel decided that after training, instead of going straight to the pub for a bit of socialising, he wanted to go to a music shop he had spotted nearby. I agreed to go with him but only for 30 minutes and then we would meet the players in the hotel bar.

Geoff was a great player and a fantastically funny man. He could make a six-hour coach trip great fun with his dry humour and his outstanding musical ability. Geoff played the ukulele, the instrument made famous in Britain by George Formby in his films of the 1930s and 1940s, and was also very handy on several other instruments including the piano and the accordion. He is a very talented musician.

Geoff's eyes lit up as we approached the music shop, and he walked in like a child in a sweet shop. There, on the wall of the shop was a fabulous ukulele on display. Geoff was instantly mesmerised and, without asking permission from the manager, Geoff pulled it off the wall and started going into full-on George Formby mode. Strumming feverishly to a stunned audience of me and the shop manager, Geoff got carried away and his huge muscular frame was no match for the ukulele, which broke in half and was left dangling in pieces by its strings. Before the manager could say anything, Geoff turned to him and said, "You're lucky I never bought that. It's fucking rubbish," and bolted, leaving me facing the manager, who said "That ukulele is 500 dollars." With Geoff well down the road by now, I said "Don't look at me, I haven't touched it," and I ran out of the shop looking for Geoff!

Gareth Jenkins, the Llanelli flanker, was another player on that tour who is another fantastic person on a rugby trip. Unfortunately, he had got injured in the last game before we went to North America, so to check his fitness he had a run-out at Waterton Cross in Bridgend where South Wales Police play.

Gareth was upset at picking up this untimely injury just before going on tour, and was desperate to come up with a ruse to get on that plane, so we all agreed to help him pass his physical tests (which were nothing strenuous at all)! He put a bandage on his injured knee, hoping for the best, and we decided to run either side of him and support him the best we could. I think the Barbarians committee members who were there seeing if Gareth was fit to tour, must have had a few in the clubhouse bar that lunchtime because how they approved him to travel, I will never know. To be fair to Gareth, though, he managed to get through the tests with our help.

Gareth had made the tour but it was no surprise to any of the players that he pulled up injured inside the first ten minutes of the opening game in Boston, and didn't play again on that tour. That didn't stop him having a great trip, and what a trip he had! It could not have happened to a nicer bloke. He had about three weeks travelling from place to place developing a glorious a suntan with his face in permanent smile mode. Sometimes touring can be backbreaking work!

It was during a night out in Toronto that Gareth got myself and Dave Shedden, the Scottish winger, into a spot of bother. It was entirely innocent at first as we wandered from bar to bar on a night out. We ended up in a bar in the centre of the city, and we were probably a bit slow on realising it wasn't quite like the other bars we had visited. It slowly dawned on us that the bar was full of men. We decided, though, that as we already had bought a drink we would stay for a short while.

The situation got more interesting after Gareth, 'for a laugh', decided to blow a kiss at one of the men looking over at us. This, however, didn't go down well with that bloke's boyfriend, who became very annoyed. Dave and I appealed to Gareth to stop stirring things up as, by now, the bar's regulars were not at all impressed with his behaviour. There was only one exit to the bar, so myself and Dave made a break for it, but because Gareth was injured he was a lot slower than us, particularly his sprinting abilities, and he made a very undignified exit as he hobbled out of the place.

One afternoon, a 'team building' task included an international golf tournament for which Scotland was drawn against Wales, meaning Gareth Jenkins and me faced Andy Irvine and Dave Shedden with our national pride at stake. The 18-hole challenge also included the side-bet that the losers at each hole would forfeit an alcoholic drink to the winners, and after 12 holes the Scots were 12-0 ahead! The booze thankfully kicked-in on the back nine and we managed to beat the inebriated Scottish duo on the final six holes to restore some pride – not that Andy or Dave could remember a lot of it.

In 1979 I toured France with the Welsh invitational team, Crawshays, where we were scheduled to play three games. After two relatively easy games we travelled down to the south of France by train and drank it dry of beer, wine and any other booze we could get our hands on, all paid for by Crawshays. Little did we know that the third game was going to be a serious step-up in quality and would be a game of immense importance, but we were completely oblivious to this as we merrily travelled along, bottle in hand.

After arriving in southern France, and several more days of drinking and enjoying ourselves, we found out that we were the sacrificial lambs to French fly-half, Jean-Pierre Romeu's French XV, which had been put together for his testimonial game. So much for amateur rugby! Romeu was still playing for France at the time, but he was sitting in the stand for his testimonial, no doubt enjoying himself with a few drinks while taking in the game.

Unfortunately for us, the side selected, with the exception of Romeu, was pretty much their current international side, with the likes of Serge Blanco, Jean-Pierre Rives and Jean-Pierre Bastiat. We should have recognised how difficult this game would be as 42,000 fans filled the stadium to watch us take a beating! We put up a decent fight and struggled through to a huge 42-21 defeat. The French were happy to have put one over this team of Welshmen, but we were equally happy to have survived the ordeal and to have scored 21 points, after consuming so much booze on the way down.

It was in this game that Allan Martin showed his true colours, after recognising early in the proceedings that a good hiding was on the cards. He was our primary source of ball in the lineout, and saw that this game was certainly no 'friendly'. After about ten minutes, Allan let out a piercing scream during a lineout and fell to the ground in apparent agony. The physio came on to treat Allan, but the Wales and British and Irish Lion's lock had already decided that enough was enough and he had seen his chance to escape a physical hiding, he left the field before the physio could get to him!

Allan had made his mind up that he was too severely injured to carry on and later, when we came off the field at the end of the game, he was sat in the changing room with a surgical collar on, as proof of an injury caused by the opposition. However, it was no surprise a few hours later to see Allan up on his feet with no surgical collar in sight, leading the dancing in the *discotheque*, that was hosting the celebrations after the game. What a fantastic recovery!

I still wonder about how much Jean-Pierre Romeu had pocketed from his testimonial. At the equivalent of around £3 a ticket, and with 42,000 in attendance, the gate money would be around £126,000. Not a bad day for sitting in the stand, counting the crowd while having a few drinks!

Another enjoyable tour was in 1980 when I accepted an invitation to play for a World XV against Argentina, to celebrate the opening of their new stadium, *Estadio Arquitecto Ricardo Etcheverry*, in Buenos Aries. It wasn't the best 15 players in the world, but more of a representation of the nations that played competitive rugby. Mike Davis, the former-England international lock forward, was our manager for the tour, which did not get off to a great start because the *apartheid* issue was prominent. The South African players in our squad got as far as Buenos Aires airport, and were immediately sent home.

The World XV squad included John Scott, Maurice Colclough, Mike Slemen, Kevin O'Brien, Bernard Vives, Jean-Pierre Rives, Gérard Cholley, Robert Paparemborde and Jacques Fouroux. A very impressive collection of outstanding players. It proved, however, to be more of a drinking expedition than a serious rugby tour. Anything you wanted in our hotel was free, but as soon as you went outside the hotel you paid for everything, and it was expensive.

The typical day would be training with Mike Davis, who'd put us through our paces for two hours, then back to the hotel and straight to its revolving rooftop bar overlooking Buenos Aires. We spent a few hours on the *cócteles* (Spanish for cocktails) before lunch. You had to collect the receipts for drinks and then slip them under the door of Mike's room to secure your expenses. You could hear Mike's moans as he was opening up and adding up all the bills he was getting for *cócteles*. Then it was onto the evening's *cócteles* when the same process would start again.

It will not surprise you when I say our trip to Argentina was very enjoyable! The game itself was a well-contested affair in front of 45,000 spectators. There was lots of open attacking rugby, a bit like a Barbarians game, with plenty of tries, and it was great to play with some of the French lads rather than getting battered by them. The hosts ran out 36-22 winners which pleased everyone. They were happy to win in their new stadium in front of their fans, and we were ecstatic that we lasted 80 minutes.

After the match, we were travelling back to the hotel on the bus when the Argentinian Rugby Union's liaison officer, a gentleman called Carlos (as every Argentinian male seemed to be named) stood up and gave us the itinerary for the rest of that day. Part of which was a 'drinks meeting' before the official dinner taking place later for all of the players. Carlos told all the players that they must go to the Shakespeare Bar for the meeting. A few of us looked puzzled, so I innocently asked "Which bar and where is it, Carlos?" His instant reply was, "The one you and your friends have lived in all week since you arrived!" We had no idea the hotel bar had a name!

This was to be my last representative game in rugby union, my fledgling business and a desire to play rugby league were to change the direction of my career. Not a bad way to go out, on a trip to Buenos Aires on a rugby tour with a World XV and a belly full of free *cócteles* is it!

14

Cardiff Blue Dragons 1981-84

'I remember going to Ninian Park when the Cardiff Blue Dragons RL team was established. The team manager Dai Watkins had recruited Steve Fenwick, Tom David and Paul Ringer from rugby union and I was pleasantly surprised how quickly they all settled in and began to shine, which boded well for the Wales RL team. Steve was a fine rugby footballer in both codes, a reliable kicker and solid in defence.'
Jim Mills (Wales RL, Great Britain RL)

Like many Welsh rugby union players of the period, I had received a few offers to go 'North', during my career. In 1977, after a Five Nations game against England in Cardiff, Wendy and I returned home on the Sunday morning to find two men stood on our doorstep. We were now living in Groeswen, a little village near Caerphilly with 16 houses, a pub and a chapel. High up in the mountains above Caerphilly, it is well away from any main roads so they clearly were not lost and looking for directions.

You can imagine my shock when they replied to my question asking who they were and what they wanted. The first thing that struck me was their accents – one Lancashire and the other Yorkshire. These weren't the visitors a Wales international would expect at his home on a Sunday morning. They weren't autograph collectors, but they certainly wanted my signature. They were rugby league scouts – one was from Wakefield Trinity and the other from St. Helens. I invited them in and explained to them that I was not in any position to abandon my rugby union career, and also my teaching job, to go north. As a naturally competitive player I had always wondered how I would do in rugby league and if I could make a go of it, but I was at my peak and enjoying life, so going north held no appeal to me, at that time.

Four years later, at the end of the 1981 Five Nations Championship, circumstances had changed and I was seriously contemplating a switch to rugby league. I had been captain of Wales but was dropped during that campaign and it was obvious that a new group of players would be brought through into the national team. There had also been rumours of a new rugby league side being established at Ninian Park in Cardiff, the home of Cardiff City Football Club, under the guidance of the great David 'Dai' Watkins. After seeing the success of rugby league at Fulham and Carlisle, Bob Grogan, the owner of Cardiff City who wanted to increase the usage of Ninian Park as a sporting venue to boost the club's finances, had decided to supply Dai Watkins with the cash to establish a rugby league team in the capital city.

The approach to play rugby league with Cardiff City Blue Dragons came from Dai Watkins, who also approached Tom David. Dai wanted the three of us to have a private meeting, but that type of gathering was quite tricky in Wales as the three of us were well-known faces and the rumour mill would kick into overdrive within minutes. We eventually decided upon having lunch at a public house in Ogmore-by-Sea. Our clumsy attempts to keep the discussion secret failed immediately, and hilariously, as everyone in the pub knew instinctively what was happening and tried to eavesdrop on the conversation. Two Wales internationals talking to a Welsh rugby icon now managing a new rugby league team in Wales who was actively recruiting players. It did not need much working out, did it?!

The timing was perfect and I was grateful for the opportunity. I could finally fulfill my ambitions to play rugby league and also, with the Blue Dragons being based in Cardiff, I would not have to leave my home to do it, plus I could continue my business interests in south Wales. It was a chance I did not want to miss out on.

CARDIFF BLUE DRAGONS 1981-84

It came at the ideal time for me, but also for the likes of Tom David, Brynmor Williams, Paul Ringer, Gordon Pritchard, David Jones, Bob Foley, Chris Seldon, Mike Marshall, and Geoff Davies. We had all enjoyed great careers in rugby union but now wanted a new challenge – to test ourselves in rugby league – and we all made the same journey together. As business partners it was an ideal scenario for me and Tom. We could still be in business together, as well as train and play in Cardiff.

My mind was made up and I informed Bridgend RFC of my decision. I had seven magnificent years with the club and have many brilliant memories of my time at the Brewery Field. Many of my former teammates remain close and valued friends but that period of my life was at an end and I was going to play rugby league. My union days were behind me.

It certainly wasn't an easy transition and it took me quite a while to get to grips with the complicated and very different methods of league, such as running backwards at speed to get into position for the the next play. I hadn't run backwards so much in all my life! With so many of us being former union players we bonded quickly and developed our knowledge and experience of the game together. Dai Watkins also recruited a number of established league players such as Tony Karalius, Arthur Daley and Paul Woods who helped us fine-tune the skills needed in league, and we became a useful side reasonably quickly.

The head of the project, our chairman Bob Grogan, enjoyed rugby league. On a Sunday, our regular match day, Bob would frequently come to the games, both home and away, and he thoroughly enjoyed the camaraderie and the banter. When Bob first came on the team bus with us (he also sometimes flew, or was chauffeured), he would sit and chat with Dai Watkins, and assumed that when we addressed him directly, we would call him 'Mr Chairman' like the football team did. Dai Watkins also told us that we call him 'Mr Chairman', but rugby boys are a bit different. Our view was that we were all the same, regardless of ability or position in a team, and Bob was part of our team – equality was the key. It was inevitable, therefore, that one Sunday, on the way to a match, one of the players at the back of the bus shouted "Hey Bob, pass that fucking paper back to us, mate." A little startled,

Bob just accepted his fate and accepted things would be a bit different with the rugby league section of his fledgling sporting empire!

It was very apt that our first fixture in Cardiff, in August 1981, was against Salford, Dai Watkins' former team. Dai, a former Welsh international and Lions captain, had left union in 1967 and enjoyed a highly distinguished career in league with Salford, becoming a dual-code Wales international and played six times for the Great Britain team. It was a good game, even though we narrowly lost, with ex-Welsh rugby union winger Maurice Richards scoring two tries for Salford but, on a positive note, we attracted a crowd of over 9,000 at Ninian Park. It was a tremendous start for rugby league in Wales and gave us all a boost.

Whether playing home or away, Bob would always be in the bar for a few drinks after the game, but his chauffeur would actually buy the drinks for the team once Bob had handed him some crisp £20 notes. We wouldn't have that, and told Bob to get the round in himself! He was a bit embarrassed initially, but smiled and went to the bar to get the round in, returning with a big grin and a load of drinks. He loved being around us, and we loved him being there. It was such a shame he died so prematurely because I am sure he was on the verge of doing something big in rugby league. He was a great man and was sorely missed by his rugby league and football teams when he sadly passed away in 1983.

'Going North' had always been seen as a betrayal by many within rugby union in Wales, and when I switched to rugby league I saw, first-hand, the harsh treatment some players received from their former sport. While most of the league converts had been forced to move home to the north of England, it was different for me and most of the Cardiff team as we still lived and socialised in south Wales. The cruel tradition had been for those who'd taken the money and headed north to be shunned by the WRU and banned from rugby clubs in Wales. I experienced some of that and some good friendships suddenly turned sour once the move to league had occurred.

One such absurd episode occurred when the Blue Dragons were travelling to play a fixture, and we stopped in a motorway services somewhere in the Midlands. Keith Rowlands, the chairman of selectors for the WRU, was also there, with his wife, and a few of us saw them walking in our general direction, clearly not aware that we were there.

His wife saw us first, and made a point of coming over to have a chat and wished us all the best. Little did she know that Keith, on seeing us had darted off into the gents' toilets to hide from us. He kept bobbing his head around the entrance to the toilets to check if we had gone and if it was safe to come out. He believed he couldn't possibly be seen speaking to us rugby league traitors. It was a pathetic situation.

Sunday was a good day for playing rugby league as it had little competition from other major sports and also enabled rugby fans to watch union on a Saturday and league the following day. Ron Jones, the Welsh Olympic sprinter, was part of our coaching team and worked on our fitness. It was a revelation as my weight dropped, from 14 stone 10 pounds to 13 stone 4 pounds, and I had never been so fit in my life. I was now 30 years of age and had never felt better. In rugby league, the ball is in play for 78 of the scheduled 80 minutes, and you were never standing still for long. There was no waiting around for scrummages or lineouts, it was all action, and it was great to play every week.

Our training was based mainly on core fitness and strength. Some players were more committed to training than others, but we were a fit bunch. However, my big mate Tom David had devised a devilish plan for the two and a half miles pre-training, warm-up run from Ninian Park towards Dinas Powys and then back again. Tom discovered that a bus followed a similar return route so tucked some money into his running shorts and caught the bus from Dinas Powys back to Ninian Park. With such impressive times and looking as if he had hardly put in any effort, were all stunned with Tom's newly found levels of fitness. Then one day, Tom was spotted emerging from behind the bus shelter, where he'd been hiding, to board the bus back to Ninian Park. Tom was a great rugby player, with incredible strength as a ball-carrier and it was no surprise that he scored a record 29 tries for a prop forward in a rugby league season. That's a try total any back back would be proud of, but for a prop forward it was simply phenomenal.

The crowds in the rugby league heartlands took no prisoners and it was odd to be booed onto the pitch at every away game, but we eventually got used to it. It was a mini England v Wales international every weekend, as opposing players wanted to prove that rugby league was a more challenging game than rugby union and that their players were much better and more talented than union players. They particularly liked to send their views in brash terms at the ex-international rugby union players who they had seen grace their televisions for several years. Tom David, Brynmor Williams, Paul Ringer and me found ourselves on the receiving end of the boo-boys' attention on a regular basis.

In one such incident, when we were playing Batley, Tom ran onto the field wearing Paul Ringer's jersey by mistake, and couldn't understand the nasty comments he was getting from the crowd, far worse than the usual abuse. Paul Ringer's infamous sending off against England at Twickenham meant he was targeted as the Welsh villain throughout the game. Tom took the abuse and only realised at the end of the game that he was wearing Paul Ringer's jersey as it appeared in the match programme. In the clubhouse afterwards, he spent most of his time trying to convince the Batley supporters that he was 'good old Tom David' and not the 'nasty Paul Ringer', who had been wearing Tom's jersey and evaded the abuse!

We played in Division 2, and had quite a good side, but we couldn't quite manage the promotion into the top division that would have helped secure the future of rugby league in south Wales. A typical Blue Dragons line up would have been: 1, Gordon Pritchard; 2, Adrian Barwood; 3, Steve Fenwick; 4, Frank Wilson; 5, Chris O'Brien; 6, Ken Gwilliam; 7, Glen French; 8, Tom David; 9, Tony Karalius; 10, Alan Bailey; 11, Arthur Daley; 12, Paul Ringer; 13, George Nicholls. We had some great times together in the three years I played in rugby league, although the travelling up north for games could be arduous at times, especially the Cumbrian clubs of Workington, Carlisle and Barrow. The games were tough on the bodies and recovering from hard-bruising games did take some time, but I have great memories and and many stories.

In one game, away against Barrow, we faced an enormous guy called Eddie Syzmala who was a ball of muscle who took a lot of bringing down when he was in full flight. He was a giant of a man and caused us problems throughout the match due to his sheer size and strength. During a passage of play, Chris Seldon, me and David 'Dai' Barwood – who was the brother of our winger, Adrian Barwood – tackled Eddie and managed to get him down. For some unknown reason, though, Dai decided to give Eddie a friendly post-tackle punch in the eye as we were getting up. Of all the people to pick on! I couldn't believe Dai had done it! Eddie looked up at us and growled like a giant in a Hollywood film. He wanted revenge on the culprit. By then, the three of us were now in a defensive line with the rest of the team. We had surprised ourselves by how fast we had got back into position. Dai muttered quietly, "Do you think he knows who punched him?" Although we shook our heads and assured Dai that he'd got away with it, Chris and I had no doubt that Eddie knew who the wrongdoer was because we had already pointed at Dai's head to help Eddie identify the culprit. We wanted to avoid any part in Eddie's retribution! Dai then spent the rest of the game avoiding Eddie to save his good looks and possibly his future in rugby league.

Controversy used to surround Paul Ringer in both rugby league and union and, to be honest, it was part of Paul's make-up and made him the character he is in life. At the end of one season, the night before the Challenge Cup Final at Wembley, we played Fulham at Stamford Bridge, Chelsea FC's ground in London. With so many league fans in London that weekend many of them had come to watch our game. It was a cracking match and we played very well, beating Fulham who were a good side in those days. After our deserved victory we were determined to enjoy the post-match celebrations, but they got slightly out of hand and created another chapter in the Paul Ringer story.

We were talking to some fans who were having a good old drink in the Stamford Bridge bar when a guy, who happened to be a warden at Brixton Prison, kindly asked about our plans for the evening and invited us to the Brixton Prison Social Club for a beer and a disco. He said that the beer in the club was 40p a pint! We could not believe our luck – 40p! – and felt like we had hit the jackpot for the rest of the night. Minutes after arriving, an incident occurred at the bar, and one of the off-duty prison staff came over, shouting: "Who's in charge of this lot?" Something had kicked-off.

"It's probably me," I replied. "I'm the team captain. What's the problem?" I was then told that one of our players has just head-butted the barman, who was now covered in blood, pouring out from his nose. The offender was none other than Paul Ringer, who claimed it wasn't his fault. Things were starting to get very unpleasant in the bar and we decided to leave before things got even worse. As we travelled home we all took turns in telling Paul we were not very happy with his behaviour. At 40p a pint we were all livid for missing out on a night of cheap booze!

Paul Woods, the ex-Tredegar and Pontypool full-back and scrum-half, was another who had come into rugby league. 'Woodsy' as he was known, was an exciting recruit for the Blue Dragons, especially as, by then, he had created quite a reputation as an uncompromising player. At five foot six in height, weighing around 16 stone, and being as hard as nails, he was built like a billiard ball. Sometimes his temper would get him into trouble, but we were all glad that Woodsy was on our side and not playing against us. When making a tackle, he would line the opposing player up, in a manner resembling a flying head-butt to the chin or face of the player, but wrapped his arms around the player to convince the referee that it was nothing more than a conventional tackle. We all knew, though, that it was as illegal as hell.

After one game at Oldham, the league leaders at the time, I witnessed one of Woodsy's specials when he tackled Bob Mordell, the Oldham forward, who was a great friend of mine from our college days in Borough Road. Bob looked badly shaken up after Woodsy had delivered another of his distinctive tackles just before half-time, and was carried off on a stretcher. At the end of the game, when I went to see how he was, Bob was still in a bad way in the treatment room, accompanied by his concerned wife. As captain of the Blue Dragons, and as a friend, I offered my apologies and he nodded his head in appreciation, but Bob's wife, Jayne, who was at college with the both of us, wasn't so accepting and gave me a sharp slap across the face. She held me responsible for Bob's injury, and as captain, I was.

Paul 'Woodsy' Woods was a great player to have on your side and he worked hard to nurture his 'hard man' image. As a scrum-half he was always at the centre of the action but possessed a quick temper and violence could escalate rapidly, in training with his teammates or during a game against the opposition. One year we drew Widnes in the Challenge Cup, with the game to be played in Cardiff. At that time Widnes were top of Division One and a superb side. It was an excellent opportunity for us to show our talents against the best team in England. The Widnes scrum-half was a young man called Andy Gregory who found himself facing our destructive dynamo, Paul Woods. It was a great, fierce battle and the pair were constantly giving each other verbal abuse.

Despite his tender years, Andy was a very confident man and decided to take the verbal exchanges a bit further by goading Paul.

CARDIFF BLUE DRAGONS 1981-84

Knowing how volatile Woodsy could be, I spoke to Andy several times and tried to get him to tone it down. Andy was having none of it and delighted in telling Paul that he was too old to be playing and should retire, amongst other things. By now I was pleading with Andy to stop, but it fell on deaf ears. Eventually, Paul told Andy in no uncertain terms that he would get him next Tuesday morning, while Andy was out shopping with his missus in Widnes! Paul, a former Widnes player, said he'd seen him previously and knew where he went. That did the trick as Andy soon shut up. He could see in Paul's eyes that he meant every word. The goading was over!

For all of his reputation as a hard man, Paul was a great player who was also a rugby league international for Wales. On a few occasions I played alongside him in the second row, him at five foot six and me at five foot ten. It must have been one of the smallest second rows in rugby league history. He was a good man to have by your side whenever you got into trouble and he was great company on those long road trips up to northern England. Sadly, Paul died in 2007 aged only 57 and many former players turned up at his funeral in Pontypridd to pay their respects to the great man.

Tom David was a particular success at rugby league. In my view he was more suited to rugby league than union due to his extraordinary upper body strength. Nine times out of ten, Tom would beat his opponent and either score himself or create a gap for his support runners as his 51 rugby league career try total testified. Tom received many good offers to play elsewhere but he stayed with the Cardiff City Blue Dragons and as a partner in our business, Triple Crown Chemicals, which was very fortunate for me.

During the celebrations, in 1984, to mark the 50th anniversary of the establishment of rugby league in France, Tom and me were selected to play for a Great Britain & France v Australia & New Zealand exhibition match. It was a great experience to play in Paris, with and against some of the best players in the world.

Playing opposite me in that game was the Australian, Mal Meninga, one of the greatest rugby league players of all time. He was massive, quick and skilful, so a bit of a handful! He was by far the best player on the field and helped his side to a comfortable victory. Nevertheless, it was a great experience to play against him. Later that year, I saw photos from that game which showed me trying to tackle Mal in full flight, but it looked more like I was hanging on while he dragged me across the pitch! What a player he was.

We also played for Wales against England, and for Wales against Australia, who were the World Champions at that time. Both games were great occasions, and even though Australia outclassed us, we gave them a good game. We only lost to England by a small margin, and we earned respect from the English players who thought they were going to hammer us.

The bias against the Welsh rugby league players was clear and unrelenting, both among supporters, opposition players and, indeed, referees. During one game against Batley I was in midfield and passed the ball out wide to Adrian Barwood. A few seconds later, as I was still admiring my pass, my opposite number smashed my face with a short arm tackle. In great pain, I went down on one knee to try and recover from a clear foul when the referee ran past me. "You must have seen that late tackle, ref?" I called over to him, but he had no sympathy and his reply was classic: "You're being paid enough, now get on with it!" In other words, you're Welsh and being paid to play, unlike rugby union, so stop complaining.

I must admit that a 'red mist' descended onto me, and I spent the next ten minutes chasing my opposite number all over the field to exact revenge. Finally, my chance came and I laid him out. The crowd went berserk and wanted this Welsh so-and-so sent off. Amazingly, the referee said, "That's one each, but the next one gets sent off." I was genuinely amazed by the decision and came to the conclusion that English rugby league referees were not as bad as I thought!

Ronnie Campbell was one of the best referees in rugby league and was involved in many infamous incidents, one involving a true legend of the game, Jim Mills, the Aberdare-born forward, renowned as being the hardest man in rugby league, and nobody would argue with that if they had any sense. David Watkins told me some fabulous stories about Jim, and explains why he remains one of the most celebrated characters of the game.

The best story for me was that of Jim and Ronnie was when they bumped into each other in one of Jim's nightclubs in St. Helens. Jim owned two nightclubs in the area, and all rugby league players were allowed in for nothing, which was a very generous gesture. Off the field, Jim is a gentleman and a loveable character who gets on with everyone. On the rugby league field, he was a different person and certainly earned his hard-man reputation. Ronnie, seeing Jim in the club, called him over and said, "I see you're playing for Barrow on Sunday. I'm reffing, so what do you say about us going up together, and share the petrol money?" Jim was turning out for Barrow as part of his recovery from an injury and Widnes, his club, wanted him to get some game time in before returning to their team. "Yeah, sure," said Jim. On Sunday morning, Jim picked up Ronnie in his car, and drove to Barrow. As they neared the ground, Ronnie said: "Wait, Jim, you had better drop me off here, it wouldn't look good me turning up in your car, because the opposing fans might assume I would be biased towards them, you know." Jim was ok with this and dropped Ronnie off a safe distance from the ground and headed to the ground.

Right from the start of the game the opposing side couldn't wait to play against Jim Mills, and some wanted to test themselves out against the well-known hard man. He did not disappoint them, or their supporters who screamed for Jim to be sent off on several occasions! Some calls were merited, some not, but the game was getting out of control. By now, Jim had laid out a few opposing players and had also taken a few knocks himself. After yet another violent incident, Ronnie Campbell blew the whistle and called Jim over to lecture him on his behaviour. Their opposing team's supporters were loving the fact Jim was getting a talking to. Ronnie said to Jim, "Don't laugh when I am talking to you, as the crowd will not be happy about it. You have to stop knocking people over, or I will have no alternative, you will have to walk." In a flash, Jim replied, "Yes, and if you do, I won't have to walk anywhere near as far as you'll have to walk!" Needless to say, Jim stayed on until the end of the game and gave poor Ronnie a lift home.

Jonathan Davies, 'Jiffy' as he is known by many, was an exceptional talent in both codes, and when he first signed for Widnes from rugby union they initially only played him in second team games because of the potential abuse in away games from their opponents' supporters.

Jiffy was playing for Widnes 2nd XIII against a Hull 2nd XIII that included Frankie Foster, who was renowned for dishing out punishment when he was in the mood. A scrum was called, and as the two sets of forwards engaged, Frankie looked up and said: "If you come down the blindside, Davies, and I will rearrange your face." Jiffy turned to the referee and asked: "What are you going to do about that then?" The referee responded with, "Well, it's like this. He hasn't actually committed any sort of foul as yet, so I can't penalise him but, if I were you, I wouldn't go down the blindside, Davies!"

The demise of Cardiff City Blue Dragons started when, with lower attendances and financial issues, we moved grounds to the Brewery Field in Bridgend, becoming the Bridgend Blue Dragons. As it turned out, the move would last a single season before the rugby league team came to an end. Unfortunately, due to injury, I did not play for the club in its last season.

I had been suffering from a knee problem for quite a while and it all came to a conclusion when I was holidaying in the south of France with my family. I decided to teach my daughter, Kate, who was six at the time, how to dive correctly. Standing on top of a rock, looking out to the Mediterranean, I told Kate to watch me do it so she could copy the technique. but my plan totally backfired on me. I flexed my knees and pushed off the rock and, with my arms fully extended, dived into the sea. I immediately felt a sensation in my knee that wasn't good. Something had broken or snapped – I wasn't sure which.

I didn't panic, at first, but as my feet hit the bottom of the sea bed, I immediately felt an incredible pain in my knee, the like of which I have never experienced before. It was so intense I thought I was about to pass out. I swam back up to the surface but I began to sense that I could drown. Luckily, a Scottish man by the name of Renwick who was staying in the same hotel as us, ran to help me as he could see me struggling and thrashing about in the water. As he rescued me, then guided me back to the beach, he recognised who I was and kept saying how funny it was that our surnames were almost identical. I have to be honest, though, I was in so much pain and fearing I was going to drown I did not find it very funny at all!

I soon realised that my knee was locked in a bent position and to get back to my hotel I had to hop along, with my new Caledonian friend to assist me on my way. I knew I had to get back to Wales as soon as possible and seek urgent medical treatment as I could hardly walk. Luckily, my knee being bent didn't impact much on my driving ability so we packed up immediately and headed for home. I didn't even change out of my bathers!

I was operated on a few days later and my knee was restored to working order but my days of playing rugby at a competitive level were over at the age of 34. I did play a few charity games, but I didn't fancy the contact of professional rugby with a dodgy knee. I was so fortunate to have had such a great career and loved every single minute of it. If I have any regrets is that the Blue Dragons never quite achieved promotion from Division 2, as that would have capped it all off. However, I am still very content with my time in rugby league. It was a very memorable period of my life with great people, which I enjoyed very much, and I proved to myself and others I could switch codes and play rugby league to a reasonable level.

15

Reunited with Union

*'Steve is a great laugh and great company, but more importantly, a player
I would go to war with.'*
JPR Williams (Wales, British & Irish Lions)

I had no experience in team management or coaching, and it wasn't an area I felt too comfortable going into when I was first asked. My professional career was going well, but I had a want to get back into rugby. Having been captain of most of the teams I'd played for, I acknowledged that an element of 'coaching on the field' had been a personal strength. Players should lead their team by example if they can, and be able to change playing styles and approaches as the need arose. As a captain, I was certainly not a loud vocal captain, urging the troops into battle, but I would speak my mind if required and show in my play what I expected from my teammates.

In October 1992, Bridgend RFC, via its chairman, Huw Ceredig, asked me to come on board as backs coach. Clive Norling the former-referee was director of rugby at the club and was very supportive. I remained backs coach, alongside ex-Bridgend and Wales star, Gerald Williams until January 1994. I knew Gerald well from our playing days, and I hoped that we could get the most out of the squad of players that we had. The team had some real talent with a backline littered with Welsh internationals, including Matthew Back, Glenn Webbe, Gwilym Wilkins, Gareth Jones, Gareth Thomas, Dafydd James and Robert Howley. Some real star names. The biggest challenge we faced was continually losing players to clubs with more financial clout. Bridgend RFC had changed from being a leading club to a feeder club and it became very hard to compete against the clubs with much deeper pockets and better facilities.

At the start of 1994, I became Chief Executive of Bridgend and became more involved with the administrative, off-field activities, of generating revenue and managing the staff but I still stayed involved with coaching, by assisting the backs. Through my business contacts, I brought in quite a bit of sponsorship to the club, which was of great benefit, but the results on the field were not as we all wanted and I was relieved of my duties at the end of the 1995-96 season. I was disappointed to be asked to leave, but it has not changed my warm feelings for Bridgend RFC, which is a club that gave me so much.

In 1997, I was approached by Newport RFC to assist Steve Jones, the ex-Pontypool hooker and a great friend, with the coaching. I learnt a lot from Steve. He had more experience of coaching and I was pleased to support him as the backs coach. Professional rugby was still in its early stages and, as with my time at Bridgend, we faced similar challenges. It was a strange period to be involved with rugby in Wales because although money had been involved on a small scale, going professional was a real eye-opener for Welsh rugby culture. Newport didn't have the strength in depth of many of the top clubs in Wales at the time, such as Llanelli, Pontypridd, Neath and Cardiff, so although Steve Jones and myself tried our best, the playing strength wasn't great and, if we were totally honest, our coaching could have been better during the period we were there.

The side was captained by Ian Jones, who had been at the club for many years, and we had other players with considerable experience at that level, such as Shaun O'Connor, Ian Gough, Rod Snow and Jan Machacek. We had good players, but we didn't have the biggest squad so, as the inevitable injuries mounted up during the season, we relied heavily on the youth team, with players such as Matthew J Watkins, Leigh Faulkner, Neil McKim and Chester Robinson breaking into the 1st XV. Watkins, in particular, went on to have a great career and it was heartbreaking when he passed away so young.

We enjoyed good wins, both home and away, in the domestic Welsh league and also in European competition, which was an exciting new venture for Welsh rugby clubs. Our season highlight was beating

Pontypridd in the quarter-finals of the Welsh Cup at Rodney Parade. Ponty had a dominant side at that time, so we narrowed the pitch by ten yards as we felt it improved our chances. It was a tough encounter but Shaun O'Connor kicked a late drop goal for us to edge the match 29-27. In the the semi-final we had a few injuries and Mark Davis came out of retirement to play prop for us, illustrating the weakness of our squad, and we were soundly beaten by Ebbw Vale. We also had a great European Cup win, at home against Clermont Auvergne, before being roundly beaten in the away fixture, but picking up a win against them was great for the fans and the club.

There were some excellent people at Newport RFC, both on and off the field. With such fine people as Dai Watkins, Martyn Hazell, and Tony Brown at the helm, it was a shame that we didn't deliver what they deserved, but it was not to be, and after one season my coaching career at Newport was at an end.

For a few years, I stepped away from rugby. There were a few offers, but nothing enticed me back. Then, in 2001, Abercynon RFC, who were in the second or third tier of Welsh rugby, spoke to me. I was approached by the club through Swansea, Wales, and St. Helens, prop forward, Stuart Evans, who turned out to be a great friend inside and outside of rugby. Stuart was 22 stone and not someone to mess about with.

I always thought that coaching would influence performance by at most 20%. The other 80% comes from the player's abilities to change the game with their talent. The players at Abercynon were the opposite of what I'd experienced, being 80% influenced by coaching, and only 20% reliant on their raw talent. It made the role of coach much more influential, and far more interesting.

There is always a level of change that every new coach tries to bring to a squad of players. Some players can adapt to change and go along with it, depending on their age and attitude. Change is a huge challenge for players to take on board, but my time at Abercynon really opened my eyes to the possibilities of coaching. The team had been successful at their level, but had lost a few key players to other clubs, so this new era with new coaches with fresh ideas was a challenging time for all. We trained twice a week, with Stuart taking the forwards, and I took the backs. We would then bring both groups together for a session to work as a team rather than as two separate groups. As

Stuart and I were former internationals with high expectations, the standard of play, at times, could frustrate but, in general, the players tried their best and that's all we could ask of them as coaches.

It was apparent from the beginning that the old regime at Abercynon was unhappy about change, even though it was essential if the club was to regain its glory days. Unfortunately, some of the committee and some former players who had a big say in the running of the club, couldn't let go of things and began to interfere in the coaching and the selection of the team. Stuart and I soon began to notice things going on behind our backs, which put us in a difficult situation.

On one occasion we were in the changing room before a home game and I noticed two players we hadn't selected getting prepared to play. When I spoke to them, they said that certain people on the committee had told them they were playing! This was humiliating for myself, Stuart and the rest of the players, just 30 minutes before kick-off. We regained control of the situation by replacing those two players with our original selections, but it sadly wasn't the only example of being undermined by certain people and ex-players at Abercynon.

Later that season we had a cup match at Pontarddulais RFC in Carmarthenshire. It was arranged that we would all travel by coach, but three of the players stated they were going by car and would meet us there. Two of the three were key players for us but, little did we know at the time, that these players were scheming with the usual trouble makers at the club, involved in the selection process, and had now decided to try and ruin our any chance of winning the game. The strategy was that we would lose due to the loss of these talented players, and it would be another reason to get rid of Stuart and me from the club, so they could regain total control once again.

One of the three was our scrum-half who, surprise surprise, didn't turn up. He was a significant loss to the team, but it made my day when Stuart and me, 30 minutes after kick-off, heard his voice on the phone in conversation with the ring leader who'd planned the whole thing and was standing quite close to us. When our AWOL player asked how the game was going, and what the score was, he must have felt pig sick because the last-minute replacement scrum-half was having a blinder. In the first 20 minutes he had already scored two tries, and spurred us on to a well-deserved victory. Abercynon RFC were through to the next round of the cup and the plotters' 'master plan' was in tatters!

I think the final straw was having to borrow a tight head prop forward from Caerphilly RFC's 2nd XV because our tight head prop had to drop out of the match two hours before kick-off because his wife had made him stay at home to 'await delivery of a new washing machine' that was expected that day! After that incident, Stuart and I decided to go to pastures new. My period at Abercynon RFC was also an eye-opener into how committees had different approaches to running a rugby club and their respective roles, whether they focused on the administrative and commercial aspects or whether they openly, or covertly, interfered with the selection of the team. Those committees that try to do both create a 'mission impossible' for the coaching staff, who should be enabled to run the team affairs as they see fit, within agreed financial parameters.

My mind was made up. After three roles at three different rugby clubs, that line of employment was not for me. Steve Fenwick would never again be a chief executive, team manager or coach of a rugby club. I will never regret the experiences and met some good people, but it was too political for me with too many people pulling in different directions and pursuing their own agendas. I am glad I gave it a go, and I left with no bitterness at all, just a new respect for those who do work in those key roles in rugby.

16

Talking Rugby

'With his distinctive blonde mane, skill, rugby intelligence, and a
miraculous ability to be in the right place at the right time, Steve was an
integral part of the great Welsh XV of the 1970s I grew up supporting.
Now, 40 years later, still instantly recognisable and with his place in the
pantheon of Welsh rugby assured, he remains totally unaffected by his
legendary status and is delightful company with his incredibly dry wit
always to the fore. It's been a pleasure and a privilege to have got to have
known Steve as well as I have.'

Phil Steele (Newport RFC, BBC Wales broadcaster)

After retiring as a professional rugby player, partly due to an
unfortunate knee injury and partly due to, at 34, being too old, I
was left with a massive hole in my diary. I'd been fully immersed in
rugby for nearly 20 years, with every week of my life governed by the
needs of rugby, and now I had a lot of time on my hands, especially
at weekends. The routine of training on a Monday, playing on a
Wednesday, training on a Thursday and playing at the weekend was in
my blood. What was I going to do next?

New experiences present opportunities for a different life and I was
happy to see what my new life offered. Luckily, I was still in work five
days a week with my own business, but would I just go and watch
rugby at the weekends or find something else to fill my time?

DRAGONS AND LIONS

One of my first experiences of being an ex-player was to fulfill my promise to Wendy, who had suffered, for so many years, the life of being married to a full-time rugby player. I had promised her that, when I retired, we would go and see an international rugby match, so Wendy jumped at the chance of a weekend away in Paris to see a France v Wales match. It was surreal to find myself, as a supporter, following the Welsh XV in the Five Nations Championship. It was very apt also that she chose that game as it brought back memories of my first Wales cap back in 1975. Now, in 1987, I was going back as a fan.

I was used to everything being organised by the WRU, but going as a fan proved to be a totally different and enjoyable experience, from start to finish. We caught the ferry from Swansea to France and then drove to the hotel in the middle of Paris. After seeing Windsor Davies and his friends from the classic film, *Grand Slam*, filmed in 1977, I began to see what this trip to France was all about. The Welsh fans thought it was funny to see me travelling with them on the ferry, and not flying over on a plane. Wendy found a spot near the bar, and the fans started to surround me with their witty remarks and I joined in. They were brilliant and we all were having a great time.

We quickly discovered that there was a large group of supporters from Llantwit Fardre, who were exceptionally well oiled. With me being an ex-Beddau player, and only one mile separating the two villages, I had a feeling it might be an extremely long few hours on the ferry! Sure enough, between the numerous offers of a drink from several Welsh supporters, even some Llantwit Fardre supporters, I found myself drinking merrily and thinking that being a supporter wasn't a bad thing at all. Wendy had seen enough and quickly relieved me of the car keys I had in my pocket. As an experienced rugby wife she could see what has happening. I have never been a 'shots man' and prefer beer, lager or stout. So, foolishly, after politely refusing a pint the offers changed to "What about a small one, Steve!" and the gin and whisky began to flow. Wendy knew what was happening and, sure enough, she was dead right in her assumption that I was on my way to being well and truly sozzled.

Luckily for Wendy and me, upon arrival in France, a milkman from Llantwit Fardre assisted my 'walk' back to the car. My next recollection was my head banging against the passenger side window of the car, and seeing the Eiffel Tower looming in the distance. Wendy had driven us into the city but she needed a bit of help in finding our hotel, located on the Champs-Élysées, and it was more through luck than judgement that we eventually found it, and the car park. What a relief that was, especially for Wendy.

I was starting to recover from my over indulgence on the ferry, and we decided to have a quiet evening in the hotel bar and surrounding area. We met several people we knew from the rugby fraternity and it was a nice feeling not to be a bag of nerves the night before an international. That night while we were out, we received an invitation to attend a pre-match cheese and wine party starting the following morning. The invite came from Gren Suchecki and his friends from my golf club in Pontypridd. Gren had played for Porth and Pontypridd RFC for many years, and we were delighted to accept his kind invitation as we had no plans for that morning.

You can imagine our surprise when we went to the party, and we were each given a glass of wine, with no cheese in sight. I asked where the cheese was and was told that they couldn't get any cheese, so it had turned into a wine party! I was enjoying my role as a Welsh supporter, and I realised what I had been missing for all those years.

It was a lovely sunny day and we enjoyed the colourful journey to the *Parc des Princes* stadium where we found our seats for the game. There was a good mix of Welsh and French fans around us and it wasn't long before I was being noticed. The French fans, especially by those in the row of seats behind us, called out, "Eh, Fenwick!" as they waved their leather bags of wine, which it seemed every French fan had in their hands. It soon became apparent that they were offering me a drink. "How generous," I thought. "It would be rude not to!"

As the wine began to flow, my mind wandered to the players in the changing rooms beneath us, deep in the stadium, and thought how the Welsh players would be anxious and worried about the game and here I was, in the stand, passing around the wine bags, and forging friendships between both sets of fans. Although France beat Wales 16-9, a Welsh defeat hardly ruined our celebrations, which went on into the Paris evening and finally back at our hotel. It was a fabulous weekend and I promised myself a few more of those trips abroad. Wendy, though, was not too fussed on going back to France in the near future. I can't imagine why!

Things do seem to happen to us in France. Years earlier we had decided to go camping on the *Côte d'Azur*, and ended up near St. Tropez in our little tent. We had arrived early in the morning, having driven through the night, and I was utterly exhausted so we stopped and set up camp. The sun was beating down, and outside the tent a voice boomed through the canopy, "Monsieur!" I got up, opened the tent and saw this massive bearded man on a pushbike. I explained to the man that we wanted to stay for another three nights if possible but his mind seemed to be elsewhere. "Is your name, Fenwick?" he asked. "Yes," I replied. He smiled and said, "Me, Jacques. The prop for St. Tropez." He was a friendly guy and we chatted for a while, after which he said we could stay as long as we wanted.

That night we went to the clubhouse on the camping site and I went to the bar to order a couple of drinks. "Jacques says no charge" the barman told me. "Oh no!" I thought to myself. I had rationed £8 a day to last us the trip, and I couldn't afford to pay a large bill on the last day! The next thing I knew was that Jacques had arranged for five Toulon players including Jacques Fouroux (then, the captain of France), and Christian Carrère, the French international flanker to come to the clubhouse! We had several drinks, and the next thing I remember was being asked to play for Toulon full-time. Another few glasses of wine and I might well have signed for them! As rugby was still an amateur game at the time, I naively asked them what job would I do if I signed. You wouldn't have to work, or we can find you a part-time job, they replied. Amateur rugby in France was clearly different! It was an excellent opportunity for me, but with business commitments at home and Wales doing well, I decided that it was not the time to move abroad.

The relationship with Jacques, the St. Tropez prop, didn't end there. When the holiday was over we went to pay the bar bill, and we were told, again, "Jacques, says no charge!" What a generous guy, and a huge relief for Wendy and me. Several months later, the day before Wales were due to play France at the Arms Park, I received a phone call from Jacques from St. Tropez. "Steven! Can you get me eight tickets for the game?" The match had been a sell-out for a few weeks so I called in as many favours as I could and managed to get all eight tickets for Jacques. After all he'd done for me it was the least I could do for him.

TALKING RUGBY

Following my retirement from rugby, both playing and coaching, speaking at rugby dinners and attending rugby-related presentations have became my primary attachment to rugby in general. It is incredibly nice to meet former friends and associates from the rugby world, past and present, and it also gives me and my family a chance to see different parts of the world.

An instance of this was when me, Wendy, and my son, Siôn, travelled to Queensland, Australia. It was a fabulous family trip, and we were in Brisbane for ten days. We were treated royally by the Aussies involved with the function being held at Ballymore Stadium where I had played for Wales against Queensland back in 1978.

My opening gambit as a guest speaker was a risky one. My experiences playing Queensland and the biased referee, JR Burnett – who was now deceased – was not a good one. He had tried his very best to sabotage us that day in 1978, and those memories and emotions came flooding back. One of the stands in the stadium had been named after the referee, so when I said that, as a Welshman who played in that match, Burnett had now found his proper place under 200,000 tons of concrete, it was a risky opening! Luckily for me, it went down well with the audience, who had known him for years. It was lovely that the after-dinner speech enabled me to take my family to Australia, see some old friends and acquaintances while we were there, and have a fabulous holiday.

Another invite led me to Azerbaijan, not a well-known rugby nation, located between Russia and Iran on the banks of the Caspian Sea. I had a phone call from an English friend called Ian, who asked me where I was. It was 2015, and I happened to be on holiday in Cyprus. When Ian heard I was in Cyprus, he replied, "Oh well. You don't have too far to go then!" He told me there was a get-together in Azerbaijan to which I was invited. The function was with a load of ex-pats working on the oil fields there, including loads of rugby people from the UK, America, New Zealand and South Africa. "The hospitality will be first class," said Ian. "I'm in," I replied.

Travelling from Cyprus to Azerbaijan wasn't as straightforward as I'd imagined. I had to cross the border at Nicosia and venture into Northern Cyprus before flying to Istanbul and then on to Georgia. After an overnight stay in a hotel in Georgia, I travelled to Baku, the capital city of Azerbaijan, for the function that was being organised by a relative of JJ Williams who was organising the whole event. Small world.

It turned out to be an unforgettable experience, for several reasons. On the plane from Nicosia to Istanbul I happened to be sat next to a large German man, who then also travelled on to Georgia. We got on well, and I asked him where he was going, and it turned out he too was going to Baku for the same rugby function. We even stayed in the same hotel in Georgia. He was good company, and we decided to go for a meal in the evening before flying on the following morning to Baku on the same flight. A phone call from the organisers of the function said that a man would meet me in reception to take our passports and get us the required visas for Azerbaijan.

Sure enough, the man turned up, and demanded $500 each for the visas! I was gobsmacked and told him where he could stick the $500, which was somewhere uncomfortable. Then it dawned on me that I didn't fancy being stuck in Tbilisi for the foreseeable future, so common sense prevailed. We went to the nearest bank, and I prayed I had enough in my account to cover it. Luckily I did and begrudgingly paid him the $500.

I then spoke to the organiser on the phone, explained my unhappiness about the costly visa and asked for the visa payment to be refunded by them. The organiser assured me that as soon as we met up in Baku, he would pay me back, which he did. The function went well, and it was a great experience being in a region that straddles Eastern Europe and the Middle East, but you always felt you were being observed. An authoritarian regime was running the country, and I got the feeling that the secret police were never too far away.

There was also an extremely social and memorable function back in Cyprus. It was at the British military base in Episkopi, near Limassol which is home to a lot of ex-pats of many nationalities. The military's hospitality was superb. Wendy and I were treated regally all day, starting with a chauffeur-driven car to and from Episkopi. The function lasted all afternoon and late into the evening. Some unfamiliar drinking games left me in a sorry state, but luckily we had the chauffeur drive us back; otherwise, poor Wendy would have had to have saved me again!

With these events, be it speaking or presenting awards you never known what you are letting yourself in for, but there is rarely a dull moment. I was once invited to a rugby club in the English Midlands, where I sat next to the President of the Rugby Football Union, Micky Steele-Bodger, who lived locally and was a member of the club. It was a very jolly evening and a lot of alcohol was being consumed. Halfway through my speech I heard raised voices that were getting louder and louder. The atmosphere changed quickly as swearing and threatening gestures were being exchanged between guests on two tables at the back of the room.

The RFU President apologised to the other guests for the disturbance and appealed to those people involved to show some respect to the rest of us. His appeal, however, fell on deaf ears and the situation began to turn violent as a huge brawl broke out. I was driving back to Caerphilly that night, so I quickly curtailed my speech so I could make a sharp exit. "Have you got my envelope?" I asked Micky Steele-Bodger, anxious to leave as soon as possible, but to my great surprise and with the fight ongoing at the back of the room, the RFU President asked me to stay on and draw the raffle, as guest speakers normally did!

I couldn't refuse, but that was the quickest raffle I ever drew! With scuffles now turning into an all-out brawl, I shook hands with the dignitaries, wished all who could hear me the very best for the future, and headed for the car park. I got into my car just in time as, when I looked back to the club while reversing, I could see the emergency doors burst open as the fight – now involving around 50 or 60 people – spilled outside, like the famous brawl scene in *Blazing Saddles*. It wasn't the first time I'd witnessed that sort of thing because the longer the drinking session, the more likely it is for a fight to erupt. I always try to deliver my speech as soon as possible during the evening to avoid the 'after-dinner handbags' and save me from a few black eyes in the process.

There was another occasion when I was invite to speak in Ulster, on the same weekend when the Newport Gwent Dragons were playing over there. The President of the club was a lovely man, of very few words. He was abrupt and got right to the point when we shook hands: "Steve, don't try and be clever like the last Welsh guest we had here, who let us down badly." I know the ex-Welsh international he was referring to, who had been there two years previous. He had got so drunk in the hotel before the game, he was absolutely 'blotto', by the time he delivered his after-dinner speech. Not only did he rack-up a considerable bar bill at the Stormont Hotel, he was so smashed that he was borderline incoherent and the packed room of rugby supporters and committee members was not at all impressed, especially when they had to take him back to the hotel early.

My clear instruction from the President of the club was not to try and be too clever: "Just tell a few jokes, tell a few stories and sit down!" Funnily enough, I did what I was asked and it went very well. There is nothing quite straightforward in Ireland, and whether you go as a golfer, visitor or as a rugby player, you never know what to expect while you are there. It is one of my favourite places to visit, and it was the games between Wales and Ireland in which I scored more points than any other rugby team at international level.

I really enjoy the after-dinner speaking and the numerous Q&A evenings I'm invited to attend. They enable me to keep in contact with the rugby world, whether that be the clubs, the supporters or my former teammates and adversaries. That knowing look of comradeship and mutual respect that sparkles in the eyes of old friends as we meet up in clubhouses or hotel function rooms means everything to me. Rugby without the social side isn't worth contemplating and for as long as I'm invited, I'll be making journeys across Wales, and beyond, to enjoy the company of those who love rugby as much as I do.

Epilogue

There's no getting away from it. I'm a very fortunate man to have enjoyed such a happy and successful life, being able to do what I loved most and living in a part of the world that means so much to me.

When I pop down to my local pub, the White Cross which is situated high above Caerphilly in the village of Groeswen, and sit in the beer garden I can look out across the valley and see so many places that played an important part of my life – the area where I was born, the school playing fields where I first started to play rugby, and Caerphilly Golf Club where I still play occasionally. I was only three and a half when our family moved to Nantgarw and I've lived in Groeswen, barely a mile and a half away, for over 40 years. The site of my old grammar school isn't too far, as is the school where I taught PE, and Taff's Well RFC, where I started my club rugby, is just a couple of miles in the opposite direction.

As I sit and take in the glorious views, memories of my childhood come flooding back and I think of those people who shaped my life and how rugby has changed since those carefree days of my youth and those thrilling years when I played rugby at the highest level. Those memories are important, as some of the many items I accumulated along my rugby journey, such as my Lions shirt, were destroyed when a fire destroyed Taff's Well RFC's clubhouse in the late 1990s. Thankfully, I still have many mementoes from my rugby career, but losing such treasured possessions was a blow. The clubhouse was rebuilt and is a testament to a great club that remains close to my heart and I always enjoy popping by for a pint and a chat with old friends.

Since my retirement from coaching I have remained an avid spectator of rugby and follow the progress of both codes. From my vantage point of having played both games, and my time as a rugby union coach and administrator, I have noticed that the two games have been heading in different directions over recent years, with RL arguably achieving more success.

DRAGONS AND LIONS

The 1970s were a great time, on and off the pitch, for Wales' top 16 clubs who competed in the *Western Mail*'s informal Merit Table, along with the WRU's prestigious Welsh Cup competition, the final of which was invariably played in front of a capacity crowd at the Arms Park.

The demise of the Merit Table was a real blow to the elite 16 clubs, Welsh rugby in general and to the tens of thousands of spectators who filled the terraces every week. Where have those die-hard fans from Carmarthenshire, Glamorgan and Monmouthshire gone? In those days the local derbies were mouth-watering fixtures that produced incredible rugby in front of their fanatical fans in packed stadiums, and generated large amounts of money for the clubs.

At the same time, the Welsh clubs played regular fixtures with their English counterparts, teams like Saracens, Northampton, Moseley, Bristol, Bath, Gloucester, Coventry and Harlequins. Those games had great atmospheres and generated intense cross-border rivalries, with every game having a genuine Wales v England buzz – on the pitch and amongst the crowd.

In addition to the Merit Table, the Welsh Cup and cross-border games, the senior Welsh clubs also faced the major touring sides from the southern hemisphere and could boast of many famous victories between them. Those games also boosted the incomes of Welsh club rugby and the games were always a sell-out.

The big local derbies would easily attract crowds of 10,000 to 20,000 and the cup games even more. The Bridgend v Cardiff fixture, for example, would be full to the brim for midweek or weekend games, generating large amounts of income via ticket sales but with so much of the regions' income now dependent upon the fees received from satellite, cable and free-to-air television broadcasters, the need to attract large crowds is no longer the overriding priority.

The advent of professional rugby and the creation of regional sides has diminished the status of the historic club fixtures and the establishment of European cup rugby has replaced the traditional cross-border clashes, however, the total number of spectators who now follow regional sides is small in comparison to the crowds attracted to the top domestic games in the 1970s and 1980s. Conversely, Ireland's four historic regions have flourished in the modern era with very respectable attendances for their league and European cup games while Scotland has struggled, similarly to Wales. The big winners of the modern era have been the English and French clubs who have made a success of domestic and European competitions, and whose attendance figures have been boosted by regular top-class encounters.

Amazingly, though, while club rugby has been diminished and the regions have struggled to consistently compete, the Wales national team has done extremely well under since the introduction of regional rugby, with Warren Gatland delivering a second 'Golden Era' of Triple Crowns, Grand Slams, Six Nations Championships and two Rugby World Cup semi-finals.

While the merits of the structure of Welsh rugby is a matter for heated debated in every clubhouse there can surely be no disagreement that modern-day rugby lacks flowing open play and is dominated by tactical kicking. I understand why teams are coached to kick so much, and in many ways I don't blame them for using those strategies to gain an advantage, but surely the powers at World Rugby can see that their rules have lead to this situation and they need to be changed. As a former dual-code international I can appreciate the skills and brilliance of the players but I can also see why the modern kicking game is turning people, young and old, away from the game.

The other aspect of the modern game that I find incredibly boring is the monotony of 'head down' charges into the opposition's highly organised defences. Watching huge players running at each other has been part of the game since the very beginning, although it wasn't something I particularly enjoyed being involved in, but it has now become the default style of play and we seldom see the ball passed at speed across the pitch by a backline that looks to play their teammates into space, rather than into contact. The flowing open rugby that attracted me to join Bridgend has been smothered by two lines of players facing each other across the pitch, trained to smash into each other. It's trench-warfare rugby and the game is worse for it. Also, the increasing number of players suffering from serious head injuries, and the possible links to long-term brain damage needs immediate attention. Why should the health of players be put in jeopardy because rugby's rule-makers are too timid to act?

Conversely rugby league has done the opposite over the past ten years in that they have moved away from the old head down charge into two packs of forwards. They have made it more attractive as a sport and the crowds have increased to watch league at its best – fast running rugby, with clever tactics designed to utilise space all over the pitch. Fitness levels in league are fantastic and its probably fair to say that modern RL is closer to the union game that I played, when we looked to run the ball and move it quickly to the wingers. This attacking mentality has resulted in an uplift in ticket sales. Put simply, the crowds have increased alongside the quality of RL being played.

Rugby may be my passion, but my family is the most precious part of my life. Wendy and I still live in Groeswen, in the the home she bought while I was on tour in Australia with Wales in 1978. Moving house is said to be one of the most stressful aspects of adult life but I can't really comment. When I left Wales to go on tour, Wendy and I were living in one home, yet by the time I returned she had arranged everything and I simply walked through the door of our new home. We were already living in Groeswen so only actually moved around 700 yards. As house moves go, I highly recommend it!

I am so lucky to be married to such a loving, resourceful and organised wife. A nurse for over 40 years, Wendy has cared for others all her working life and is the epitome of public service. She was also a wonderfully natural mother and we have been blessed with two children who we treasure. Our daughter, Kate, graduated from Strathclyde University, Glasgow, with a MSc in Forensic Science and worked for the police service for many years. She lives in Cardiff with her husband, Craig and has recently embarked on a new career in project management software. Our son, Siôn, studied Television Production at university before spending a number of years in the music industry, and now works in energy conservation. He lives in Radyr with his partner, Danielle, and enjoys playing football and golf.

I thankfully remain in good health and make a point of exercising every day – and I'm not referring to a stroll down to the pub! I enjoy a brisk morning walk and an occasional round of golf. I also spend a lot of time in the garden which keeps me in decent shape.

I did try water-skiing once, with Derek Quinnell on the River Tywi between Llansteffan and Ferryside, but it didn't go too well. Firstly, it was an unexpected outing on the water so I was dressed in a borrowed black wetsuit that looked at least one size too small for me. Secondly, I couldn't manage to stand up and ended up being dragged across the water, on my front, my back and my side. I was all over the place and I'm certain that onlookers thought a large seal had been caught at sea and was being unceremoniously hauled back to shore. Derek was laughing hysterically at my discomfort but when it was his turn to take to the water he was just as bad! The efforts to get two British and Irish Lions to become competent water-skiers failed badly and by the time we were back on dry land, we both felt as if the All Blacks' pack had run over us, and back again.

It's not surprising, though, that the effect of playing high-level rugby for over two decades takes its toll on the body. From a fractured cheekbone to a broken collar bone, and from a dislocated shoulder to a broken nose and a broken ankle, my body has, over the years, been battered. I've had one knee replacement and am waiting for the other to be operated on but I'm still here and thankful for my good health.

Being grateful for what I have particularly strikes home when I think of my former teammates and good friends who are no longer with us, such as Gareth 'Sam' Williams, the brilliant back row forward for Bridgend, Wales and the Lions who fought his incurable condition with such dignity, the mercurial JJ Williams who left us in 2020, and John 'Sid' Dawes – to whom I owed so much – who sadly passed away in 2021.

Over the course of my life I've been grateful to win several prestigious awards, and following my quip to the Queen in 1980 I knew a gong from royalty was unlikely, but I was exceptionally honoured, in 2019, to be inducted into the Welsh Sporting Hall of Fame at a glittering event in Cardiff. Having my efforts as a rugby player honoured in such a way meant a lot, but to now stand alongside the legends of Welsh sport – many of whom were my heroes as I grew up – was a very special feeling indeed.

I am immensely proud of what I've achieved and, given the opportunity, I would do it all again. It wasn't just about playing rugby and the excitement of the big games in front of big crowds, rugby enabled me to visit so many fascinating places and meet so many wonderful people. Those friendships last for a lifetime and, no matter where I've been in the world, I've bumped into friendly faces, even those who were formidable foes on the pitch. It's always a joy to meet up with my old teammates and adversaries and as the years go by I cherish every single one.

I've come a long way since my Aunt Rose first invited me to watch Wales play on the television in her Nantgarw home. I was mesmerised from the very start and my journey has truly been a 'dream come true'. I have thoroughly enjoyed my life in rugby.

Career Statistics

Rugby Union - Club		Appearances	Points
1970-72	Taff's Well RFC	Not available	
1972-73	Beddau RFC	Not available	
1973-81	Bridgend	256	1,212
Rugby Union - International			
1972	English Colleges	1	0
1975-81	Wales	30	152
1977	British & Irish Lions	4	0
Rugby League - Club			
1981-84	Cardiff Blue Dragons	86	548
Rugby League - International			
1981-82	Wales	2	10

Index

INDEX

143

INDEX

INDEX

INDEX

149

St David's Press

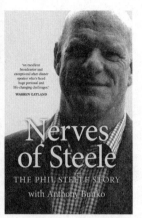

NERVES OF STEELE
The Phil Steele Story

'I've been lucky enough to get to know Phil during my time as Wales coach. He is an excellent broadcaster who genuinely wants Wales and Welsh players to excel and I respect his friendly and personal approach. I also admire the fact that he has been able to do this while facing personal and life changing challenges.'

Warren Gatland

'Phil Steele embodies all that is great about the culture of Welsh rugby. His strength of character and sense of fun are all the more impressive given some of the dark and devastating times he has endured.'

Caroline Hitt

Known to thousands of rugby fans as a knowledgeable, passionate and witty broadcaster and as an entertaining and popular after-dinner speaker, Phil Steele's confident demeanour and humorous disposition mask a life-long battle against depression and anxiety heightened by heartbreak and tragedy in his personal life. *Nerves of Steele* is a remarkable story and reveals the real Phil Steele, a man known only by his very closest friends and family.

978-1-902719-50-4	208pp	£13.99	PB
978-1-902719-53-5	208pp	£9.99	eBook

SPIKEY: 2 HARD TO HANDLE
The Autobiography of Mike 'Spikey' Watkins

'One of the most inspirational leaders that Welsh rugby has ever produced'   **Mike Ruddock**

'A great friend…also a great inspiration…he led from the front and his team mates could always rely on him when things got a bit rough, even though he'd probably started it!!'   **Paul Turner**

'No one trained harder, no one played harder…heart of a lion'   **Terry Holmes**

One of the most colourful and controversial characters in Welsh rugby history, Mike 'Spikey' Watkins remains the only player since 1882 to captain Wales on his debut, and win.

978-1-902719-40-5	251pp	£18.99	PB

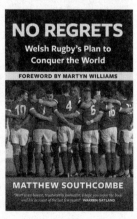

NO REGRETS
Welsh Rugby's Plan To Conquer the World

'Matt is an honest, trustworthy journalist. I hope you enjoy the book and his account of the last few years!'   **Warren Gatland**

'Having followed Wales' every move over recent years, few journalists are better-placed to chronicle the team's journey over that period of time than Matt.'   **Martyn Williams**

In *No Regrets - Welsh Rugby's Plan to Conquer the World*, acclaimed *Western Mail* rugby correspondent Matthew Southcombe reveals how the masterplan led to the 2017 tour success in Argentina, a clean sweep in the 2018 autumn internationals and, in 2019, a Six Nations Grand Slam, a record 14-game unbeaten run and a World Rugby #1 ranking. Hopes were high, amongst the squad and the nation, as the team headed to Japan with a genuine expectation winning the tournament.

978-1-902719-81-8	176pp	£13.99	PB

St David's Press

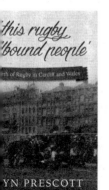

'this rugby spellbound people'
The Birth of Rugby in Cardiff and Wales

Gwyn Prescott

"...scrupulously researched [and] well written...Gwyn Prescott has given [rugby in Wales] a history to be proud of."　　　　　　　　　　　　　　　**Huw Richards, scrum.com**

"Prescott paints a meticulous picture of Welsh rugby's growth in Victorian Britain"　　　　　　　　　　　　　　　　　　　　　　　**Rugby World**

"...a fascinating piece of research and a major contribution to the history of rugby."　　　　　　　　　　　　　　　　　　　　　　　**Tony Collins**

The Birth of Rugby in Cardiff and Wales is the essential guide to the importance of rugby in Cardiff and to the significance of Cardiff to the development of Welsh rugby in the nineteenth century.

978-1-902719-43-6　　304pp　　£16.99　　PB

'Call Them to Remembrance'
The Welsh Rugby Internationals
Who Died in the Great War
(Second Edition)

Gwyn Prescott

'These pages contain an unexplored and untold tale which, from the deepest anguish of the suffering born of their unquestioning bravery, pierces the heart...This book is [an] acknowledgment of the sacrifice made by 13 Welshmen....Theirs was a sacrifice which needs to be told....Gwyn Prescott, with meticulous and sympathetic attention to detail, tells the story. This narrative is an essential record'.　　　　　　　　　　　　　　　　**Gerald Davies, from the Foreword**

It is estimated that the First World War claimed the lives of 40,000 Welshmen, all of them heroes whose sacrifice is acknowledged by a grateful nation. *'Call Them to Remembrance'*, which includes over 120 illustrations and maps, tells the stories of 13 fallen heroes who shared the common bond of having worn the famous red jersey of the Welsh international rugby team.

978-1-902719-82-5　　PB　　180pp　　£19.99
978-1-902719-90-0　　eBook　　180pp　　£19.99

St David's Press

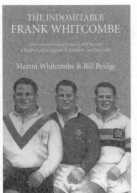

THE INDOMITABLE FRANK WHITCOMBE
How a Genial Giant from Cardiff became a Rugby League Legend in Yorkshire and Australia

'Frank Whitcombe was a rugby league cult hero in the days before there were cult heroes. A* eighteen-stone battle tank of a prop forward, he graduated from Welsh rugby union to become * pillar of the great Bradford pack of the 1940s. In the process, he became the first forward to wi* the Lance Todd Trophy, a member of the 1946 'Indomitable' Lions touring team to Australasi* and had even driven the team bus to Wembley when Bradford won the 1947 Challenge Cup Final* This book is his story - it is essential reading for anyone interested in the history of rugby and th* amazing men who made the game.'
Prof. Tony Collin

'Frank Whitcombe became a Welsh international and a Great Britain tourist. He is widely regarde* as an all-time great of rugby league.'
Fran Cotto

978-1-902719-47-4	256pp	£19.99	PB
978-1-902719-59-7	256pp	£9.99	eBook

THE INDOMITABLES
Rugby League's Greatest Tour
The 1946 'Great Britain' Tour to Australia & New Zealand

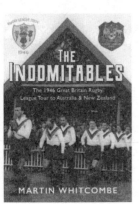

'The Indomitables were an example to all of us and set the standards for everyone tha* followed them.'
Billy Boston, former Great Britain RL internationa

'Australians admire the best in sports and the Indomitables showed they were the best. Fan* were fully engaged in every match and all the revelry that surrounded it. The papers wer* filled with news of the British players - they were celebrities and they seemed to relish tha* role. They were outstanding representatives of Britain, on and off the field.'
Pat Devery, former Australia RL internationa

Named after the aircraft carrier that took the 26 rugby players from Britain to Australi* in 1946, the Indomitables won two Test matches and drew the third to become the mos* successful tourists in British rugby league history - a feat that has never been beaten.

These were *The Indomitables* – and this is their story.

978-1-902719-702	256pp	£19.99	PB
978-1-902719-993	256pp	£19.99	eBook

St David's Press

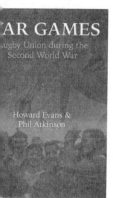

WAR GAMES
Rugby Union during the Second World War

Howard Evans & Phil Atkinson

Dedicated to 'all those in rugby who did - and who didn't - make it through those troubled times', *War Games* is a comprehensive and highly illustrated commemoration, packed with stories and statistics that for the first time chronicles the history of rugby - the men and the matches, from 'scratch' to international - during the Second World War.

Essential and entertaining reading for followers of rugby and military historians alike, respected rugby authors Howard Evans and Phil Atkinson tell the tale - meticulously and with great affection for the game they love - of those men who played for fun but who, on too many occasions, lost more than a rugby game.

978-1-902719-67-2   302pp   £25.00   PB

THE WIZARDS
Aberavon Rugby 1876-2017

Howard Evans & Phil Atkinson

'I would rather have played rugby for Wales than Hamlet at the Old Vic. To that town, Aberavon and its rugby team, I pledge my continuing allegiance, until death.'   **Richard Burton**

One of the traditional powerhouses of Welsh first class rugby, Aberavon RFC has a long, proud and illustrious history, with 50 of its players being capped for Wales, the club winning many league titles and domestic cups, and - with Neath RFC - facing the might of South Africa, Australia and New Zealand. Aberavon RFC is a great rugby club and this is its story.

978-1-902719-66-5   256pp   £19.99   PB

THE KING'S CUP 1919
Rugby's First World Cup

Howard Evans & Phil Atkinson

'An intriguing retelling of a significant but largely forgotten chapter of rugby union history, superbly illustrated.'   **Huw Richards**

'Howard is an authority on rugby's history and meticulous in his research'   **Western Mail**

After the Armistice in November 1918 – with the forces of the world's rugby-playing nations and many of their stars still stationed in Britain – and with the public desperate to see competitive rugby played again, an inter-military tournament was organised. King George V was so enthused by the proposed competition that he agreed to have the tournament named after him, and so The King's Cup was born.

The King's Cup 1919 is the first book to tell the full story of rugby's first 'World Cup' and is essential reading for all rugby enthusiasts and military historians.

978-1-902719-44-3   192pp   £14.99   PB